Ferdinand Magellan
and the Discovery of the World Ocean

General Editor

William H. Goetzmann
Jack S. Blanton, Sr., Chair in History
    University of Texas at Austin

Consulting Editor

Tom D. Crouch
Chairman, Department of Aeronautics
    National Air and Space Museum
    Smithsonian Institution

WORLD EXPLORERS

Ferdinand Magellan
and the Discovery of the World Ocean

Rebecca Stefoff

Introductory Essay by Michael Collins

CHELSEA HOUSE PUBLISHERS

New York · Philadelphia

On the cover   Atlas entitled *Theatrum Orbis Terrarum* (1570)
by Abraham Ortelius, courtesy of the Library of Congress.
Portrait of Magellan, courtesy of Archivo Oronoz, Madrid, and
Museo Torre del Oro, Seville.

Chelsea House Publishers
Editor-in-Chief   Nancy Toff
Executive Editor   Remmel T. Nunn
Managing Editor   Karyn Gullen Browne
Copy Chief   Juliann Barbato
Picture Editor   Adrian G. Allen
Art Director   Maria Epes
Manufacturing Manager   Gerald Levine

World Explorers
Senior Editor   Sean Dolan

Staff for FERDINAND MAGELLAN AND THE
DISCOVERY OF THE WORLD OCEAN
Deputy Copy Chief   Mark Rifkin
Editorial Assistant   Nate Eaton
Picture Researcher   Joan Beard
Series Design   Loraine Machlin
Production Manager   Joe Romano
Production Coordinator   Marie Claire Cebrián

9   8

Library of Congress Cataloging-in-Publication Data

Stefoff, Rebecca
Ferdinand Magellan and the Discovery of the World Ocean /
Rebecca Stefoff.
p.   cm.—(World Explorers)
Includes bibliographical references.
Summary: A biography of the Portuguese sea captain who
commanded the first expedition that sailed around the world, thus
providing the first positive proof that the earth is round.
ISBN 0-7910-1291-3
1. Magalhães, Fernão de, d. 1521—Juvenile literature. 2. Voyages
around the world—Juvenile literature. [1. Magellan, Ferdinand, d.
1521. 2. Explorers. 3. Voyages around the world.] I. Title. II.
Series.
G420.M2S74   1990   89-23950
910.92—dc20   CIP
[92]   AC

CONTENTS

WORLD EXPLORERS

THE EARLY EXPLORERS

Herodotus and the Explorers of the Classical Age
Marco Polo and the Medieval Explorers
The Viking Explorers

THE FIRST GREAT AGE OF DISCOVERY

Jacques Cartier, Samuel de Champlain, and the Explorers of Canada
Christopher Columbus and the First Voyages to the New World
From Coronado to Escalante: The Explorers of the Spanish Southwest
Hernando de Soto and the Explorers of the American South
Sir Francis Drake and the Struggle for an Ocean Empire
Vasco da Gama and the Portuguese Explorers
La Salle and the Explorers of the Mississippi
Ferdinand Magellan and the Discovery of the World Ocean
Pizarro, Orellana, and the Exploration of the Amazon
The Search for the Northwest Passage
Giovanni da Verrazano and the Explorers of the Atlantic Coast

THE SECOND GREAT AGE OF DISCOVERY

Roald Amundsen and the Quest for the South Pole
Daniel Boone and the Opening of the Ohio Country
Captain James Cook and the Explorers of the Pacific
The Explorers of Alaska
John Charles Frémont and the Great Western Reconnaissance
Alexander von Humboldt, Colossus of Exploration
Lewis and Clark and the Route to the Pacific
Alexander Mackenzie and the Explorers of Canada
Robert Peary and the Quest for the North Pole
Zebulon Pike and the Explorers of the American Southwest
John Wesley Powell and the Great Surveys of the American West
Jedediah Smith and the Mountain Men of the American West
Henry Stanley and the European Explorers of Africa
Lt. Charles Wilkes and the Great U.S. Exploring Expedition

THE THIRD GREAT AGE OF DISCOVERY

Apollo to the Moon
The Explorers of the Undersea World
The First Men in Space
The Mission to Mars and Beyond
Probing Deep Space

CHELSEA HOUSE PUBLISHERS

Into the Unknown

Michael Collins

It is difficult to define most eras in history with any precision, but not so the space age. On October 4, 1957, it burst on us with little warning when the Soviet Union launched *Sputnik*, a 184-pound cannonball that circled the globe once every 96 minutes. Less than 4 years later, the Soviets followed this first primitive satellite with the flight of Yury Gagarin, a 27-year-old fighter pilot who became the first human to orbit the earth. The Soviet Union's success prompted President John F. Kennedy to decide that the United States should "land a man on the moon and return him safely to earth" before the end of the 1960s. We now had not only a space age but a space race.

I was born in 1930, exactly the right time to allow me to participate in Project Apollo, as the U.S. lunar program came to be known. As a young man growing up, I often found myself too young to do the things I wanted—or suddenly too old, as if someone had turned a switch at midnight. But for Apollo, 1930 was the perfect year to be born, and I was very lucky. In 1966 I enjoyed circling the earth for three days, and in 1969 I flew to the moon and laughed at the sight of the tiny earth, which I could cover with my thumbnail.

How the early explorers would have loved the view from space! With one glance Christopher Columbus could have plotted his course and reassured his crew that the world was indeed round. In 90 minutes Magellan could have looked down at every port of call in the *Victoria's* three-year circumnavigation of the globe. Given a chance to map their route from orbit, Lewis and Clark could have told President Jefferson that there was no easy Northwest Passage but that a continent of exquisite diversity awaited their scrutiny.

In a physical sense, we have already gone to most places that we can. That is not to say that there are not new adventures awaiting us deep in the sea or on the red plains of Mars, but more important than reaching new places will be understanding those we have already visited. There are vital gaps in our understanding of how our planet works as an ecosystem and how our planet fits into the infinite order of the universe. The next great age may well be the age of assimilation, in which we use microscope and telescope to evaluate what we have discovered and put that knowledge to use. The adventure of being first to reach may be replaced by the satisfaction of being first to grasp. Surely that is a form of exploration as vital to our well-being, and perhaps even survival, as the distinction of being the first to explore a specific geographical area.

The explorers whose stories are told in the books of this series did not just sail perilous seas, scale rugged mountains, traverse blistering deserts, dive to the depths of the ocean, or land on the moon. Their voyages and expeditions were journeys of mind as much as of time and distance, through which they—and all of mankind—were able to reach a greater understanding of our universe. That challenge remains, for all of us. The imperative is to see, to understand, to develop knowledge that others can use, to help nurture this planet that sustains us all. Perhaps being born in 1975 will be as lucky for a new generation of explorer as being born in 1930 was for Neil Armstrong, Buzz Aldrin, and Mike Collins.

The Reader's Journey

William H. Goetzmann

●

This volume is one of a series that takes us with the great explorers of the ages on bold journeys over the oceans and the continents and into outer space. As we travel along with these imaginative and courageous journeyers, we share their adventures and their knowledge. We also get a glimpse of that mysterious and inextinguishable fire that burned in the breast of men such as Magellan and Columbus—the fire that has propelled all those throughout the ages who have been driven to leave behind family and friends for a voyage into the unknown.

No one has ever satisfactorily explained the urge to explore, the drive to go to the "back of beyond." It is certain that it has been present in man almost since he began walking erect and first ventured across the African savannas. Sparks from that same fire fueled the transoceanic explorers of the Ice Age, who led their people across the vast plain that formed a land bridge between Asia and North America, and the astronauts and scientists who determined that man must reach the moon.

Besides an element of adventure, all exploration involves an element of mystery. We must not confuse exploration with discovery. Exploration is a purposeful human activity—a search for something. Discovery may be the end result of that search; it may also be an accident, as when Columbus found a whole new world while searching for the Indies. Often, the explorer may not even realize the full significance of what he has discovered, as was the case with Columbus. Exploration, on the other hand, is the product of a cultural or individual curiosity; it is a unique process that has enabled mankind to know and understand the world's oceans, continents, and polar regions. It is at the heart of scientific thinking. One of its most significant aspects is that it teaches people to ask the right questions; by doing so, it forces us to reevaluate what we think we know and understand. Thus knowledge progresses, and we are driven constantly to a new awareness and appreciation of the universe in all its infinite variety.

The motivation for exploration is not always pure. In his fascination with the new, man often forgets that others have been there before him. For example, the popular notion of the discovery of America overlooks the complex Indian civilizations that had existed there for thousands of years before the arrival of Europeans. Man's desire for conquest, riches, and fame is often linked inextricably with his quest for the unknown, but a story that touches so closely on the human essence must of necessity treat war as well as peace, avarice with generosity, both pride and humility, frailty and greatness. The story of exploration is above all a story of humanity and of man's understanding of his place in the universe.

The WORLD EXPLORERS series has been divided into four sections. The first treats the explorers of the ancient world, the Viking explorers of the 9th through the 11th centuries, and Marco Polo and the medieval explorers. The rest of the series is divided into three great ages of exploration. The first is the era of Columbus and Magellan: the period spanning the 15th and 16th centuries, which saw the discovery and exploration of the New World and the world ocean. The second might be called the age of science and imperialism, the era made possible by the scientific advances of the 17th century, which witnessed the discovery of the world's last two undiscovered continents, Australia and Antarctica, the mapping of all the continents and oceans, and the establishment of colonies all over the world. The third great age refers to the most ambitious quests of the 20th century—the probing of space and of the ocean's depths.

As we reach out into the darkness of outer space and other galaxies, we come to better understand how our ancestors confronted *oecumene*, or the vast earthly unknown. We learn once again the meaning of an unknown 18th-century sea captain's advice to navigators:

> And if by chance you make a landfall on the shores of another sea in a far country inhabited by savages and barbarians, remember you this: the greatest danger and the surest hope lies not with fires and arrows but in the quicksilver hearts of men.

At its core, exploration is a series of moral dramas. But it is these dramas, involving new lands, new people, and exotic ecosystems of staggering beauty, that make the explorers' stories not only moral tales but also some of the greatest adventure stories ever recorded. They represent the process of learning in its most expansive and vivid forms. We see that real life, past and present, transcends even the adventures of the starship *Enterprise*.

Mutiny and Murder

On the afternoon of March 31, 1520, a fleet of 5 small ships approached the narrow mouth of a bay on the southeastern coast of South America, just north of 50 degrees south latitude. The vessels—the flagship *Trinidad*, the *San Antonio*, the *Concepción*, the *Victoria*, and the *Santiago*—were battered and worn. Since leaving their home port in Spain six months earlier, they had crossed the Atlantic Ocean, surviving violent storms and torrid tropical calms, and then coasted southward into waters unknown to European mariners. During the previous 2 months, the fleet had fought its way through more than 1,000 miles (1,600 kilometers) of some of the roughest, most treacherous seas on earth: the coastal waters of present-day Argentina, still known today as the "sea of graves" by local sailors. Those months had brought the approach of winter in the southern hemisphere, and the weather had grown steadily worse. The ships' sails had been ripped by sleet and torn ragged by screaming winds; cooking fires had been doused by seemingly endless cold rains; and below decks the bilges swirled with water from a thousand leaks.

The men aboard were in no better shape. Ice caked their clothes and beards, and their strength was exhausted from weeks of battling the tossing seas and manning the pumps to keep the ships afloat. They were in desperate need of a safe anchorage in which to rest, replenish their dwindling provisions, and repair their vessels. The foray

The first man to circumnavigate the globe, Ferdinand Magellan. After first meeting Magellan at the court of Charles I of Spain, the Dominican friar Bartolomé de Las Casas wrote of him: "[He] must have been a man of great courage, valiant in both his thoughts and in undertaking great things, although he was not of imposing presence, since he was small in stature and did not appear to be much."

into uncharted waters had left many of the sailors and officers jittery. Some of them feared that the fleet's captain-general, obsessed with the desire to find a passage westward through South America to the spice-rich Asian isles called the Moluccas, would continue to drive them south until they perished of cold or hunger or were driven to their deaths on the bleak, rocky coast.

That captain-general, the commander of the fleet, was a Portuguese soldier and navigator named Fernão de Magalhães. Called Hernando de Magallanes by the Spanish, who sponsored his expedition, he is most widely known by the French version of his name, Ferdinand Magellan. Slight of build, short, with dark hair and dark eyes, Magellan often wore a grim expression and talked little, keeping his thoughts—and his doubts, if he had any—to himself. To some of his men he seemed a distant, forbidding figure as he stalked the deck, limping from an old war wound. His unimpressive appearance had led many to underestimate him, but those who did soon discovered that this unprepossessing Portuguese was all mettle and fiber. From the time the ships had left Spain, certain officers had criticized him, mocked him, and even defied his orders, hoping to turn the crew against him, but the crew remained loyal, recognizing in Magellan a natural leader and a fair-minded taskmaster who shared the hardships of the voyage equally with those who served under him. For this brief moment, however, officers and crew were united in the hope that they had at last found a safe anchorage.

The entrance to the bay did not look inviting. It was a narrow pass through which water foamed in 30-foot (10-meter) waves. But Magellan signaled the ships to enter and, once through the pass, they floated at ease in a harbor surrounded by barren cliffs and gray beaches. Magellan named the place Port San Julián. Then, to the dismay of those who had hoped they would quickly make repairs and put out for more hospitable shores, the captain-general announced that the fleet would spend the winter at Port San Julián and resume the southward course in a few months. Rations, he added, would be cut in half in order to protect the remaining provisions, but he was certain that the surrounding countryside would provide good hunting. Once the Sabbath had been honored, Magellan ordered, the men should begin building huts for shelter on the shore.

The dissatisfied men began muttering and grumbling almost before the anchor chains had stopped rattling. A group of officers and men presented their objections to Magellan, requesting that he either guide the fleet home or make for the Moluccas by the known route—by recrossing the Atlantic, then sailing around the tip of Africa and east across the Indian Ocean. Antonio Pigafetta, a member of the expedition who compiled the most complete account of the voyage, succinctly noted what happened next: "Magellan refused to discuss the matter, and when some of the crew persisted, he had them arrested and punished. This exasperated the men still further."

A 1510 map of the Moluccas, or the Spice Islands. In the late 14th and early 15th centuries, Europe's seafaring powers were all seeking a route to the Spice Islands. Note that although the chart indicates that the islands are prosperous and heavily populated, it gives little indication of their exact location.

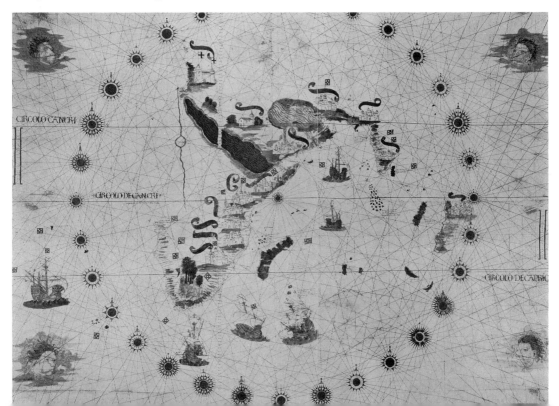

This woodcut of the Victoria, *the only ship of Magellan's fleet to make it back to Spain, appeared in the 1589 edition of the Flemish cartographer Abraham Oertel's* Theatrum orbis terrarum *(Theater of the World). At 85 tons, the* Victoria *was the second-lightest of Magellan's ships; it most likely carried 3 masts, not 2.*

The next day was Palm Sunday. The devout Magellan ordered everyone ashore to attend Mass, but three of his captains defied him. They were Luis de Mendoza of the *Victoria*, Gaspar de Quesada of the *Concepción*, and Juan de Cartagena, whom Pigafetta called "the ringleader." Cartagena had originally commanded the *San Antonio*, but his continual plotting and insubordination had forced Magellan to relieve him of his post. Although Cartagena was supposed to be a prisoner on the *Victoria*, Mendoza released him. After Mass, while Magellan shared a meal aboard the *Trinidad* with Alvaro de Mesquita, his cousin and the new captain of the *San Antonio*, the three rebellious captains laid their plans.

That night, a boatload of Quesada's men rowed silently toward the *San Antonio*. They were led by Cartagena and

Quesada; the *Concepción*'s pilot, Juan Sebastián de Elcano, also had joined the plot. To avoid detection, the
men in the boat had blackened their faces with charcoal,
and they had wrapped their oarlocks with the skins of
penguins to muffle the betraying creak of rusty iron. A
traitor aboard the *San Antonio*, Geronimo Guerra, helped
Cartagena and the others board and then capture and chain
the sleeping Mesquita.

To that point the revolt had been successful, silent, and
bloodless, but then the *San Antonio*'s master-at-arms,
Juan de Lloriaga, came on deck. Quesada ordered him to
keep quiet, but Lloriaga loyally raised the alarm, crying
out across the dark waters. The mutinous Quesada struck
at the unarmed Lloriaga with his sword; six blows were
needed to silence the master. The ship's men who remained loyal to Magellan were clapped in irons, and Quesada assumed command of the *San Antonio*. Cartagena
was given the *Concepción*.

When April 2 dawned, Magellan found three of his
ships allied against him under the Spanish captains. Only
the *Santiago*, the smallest ship of the fleet, remained loyal.
It was captained by João Serrão, a fellow Portuguese and
a friend.

It was not long before Quesada sent half a dozen men
in a boat to the *Trinidad*. They carried a message to Magellan, offering to return the ships to his command if
Magellan agreed to certain conditions. Quesada invited
Magellan to discuss the matter on the *San Antonio*. Too
wily for such a ploy, Magellan had already decided to set
a bold trap of his own, one that would require careful
timing, loyal followers, and more than a little luck. He
enlisted the aid of Duarte Barbosa, his brother-in-law and
one of the flagship's officers, and Gonzalo Gomez de Espinosa, the *Trinidad*'s master-at-arms. They seized Quesada's boat and messengers, leaving Quesada uncertain of
what had happened aboard the *Trinidad*. Magellan then
moved against the *Victoria* rather than the *San Antonio*,

*Juan Sebastián de Elcano, the
Basque pilot of the* Concepción.
It was Elcano who brought the
Victoria *back to Spain, where,
despite his participation in the
mutiny against Magellan, he was
received at the Spanish court as
a hero.*

perhaps because the *Victoria* was the smaller ship. He wrote a letter to Mendoza, inviting the discontented captain of the *Victoria* to a parley aboard the *Trinidad*.

Carrying Magellan's message, Espinosa and five cloaked sailors rowed a longboat toward the *Victoria*. At the same time, Barbosa and 15 loyal seamen slipped over the side of the *Trinidad* into a second longboat. Screened from the rebel ships by the fog and mist of the winter evening, they too approached the *Victoria*.

Espinosa and his five men were permitted to bring Magellan's letter aboard. It is said that Mendoza laughed scornfully when he read it. If so, it was his final laugh. Pretending to reach for the letter, Espinosa grabbed Mendoza, then brought a dagger out from his cloak and stabbed the rebel in the throat, killing him instantly. At that same moment, Barbosa and his men swarmed over the side and seized control of the ship.

Quesada in the *San Antonio* and Cartagena in the *Concepción* looked on in bewilderment as the *Victoria* raised anchor and began moving, but their confusion ended when the former rebel ship lined up with the *Trinidad* and the *Santiago*, blocking the harbor mouth. The odds, suddenly with Magellan, became even more precipitous in the captain-general's favor when the *San Antonio*, its anchor cables cut by loyal or reconsidering crewmen, began to drift toward the *Trinidad*. Quesada's men deserted the deck, leaving their commander standing alone, bellowing orders that no one heeded. Boarding parties from the *Trinidad* and the *Victoria* retook the *San Antonio* without bloodshed.

Aboard the *Concepción*, Cartagena glumly watched these maneuvers. He had no chance of outrunning or outfighting the four ships now arrayed against him, and when Espinosa approached in a longboat and demanded to know the ship's allegiance, Cartagena had no choice but to reply, "We stand for King Charles of Spain and for

Ferdinand Magellan as his captain-general" and to surrender his ship. With that, the mutiny was over. One
mutineer, Mendoza, had died, and Lloriaga, the loyal
master-at-arms, lay gravely wounded. All that remained
was to punish the rebels.

The motivation of the mutineers and Magellan's subsequent treatment of them remains a subject of historical
controversy. Magellan was an extremely hard-driving and
single-minded individual, and there is little doubt that he
asked more from his crew and officers than they were used
to giving. Six months at sea was a voyage of almost un-
precedented duration—Columbus's first journey to the
New World had taken about five weeks—and the entrance
into the unknown waters of the southern hemisphere
added an even greater element of uncertainty and risk.
Few of the crewmen had been informed of the exact nature
of the expedition when they signed on; most initially had
only vague notions, gleaned from dockside gossip and ru-
mor, about the voyage's true purpose. The captain-general's navigational skills to that point had given no reason
for confidence—the ships had been becalmed for weeks
under a broiling sun because of Magellan's insistence on
taking an unproven route along the coast of Africa, and
now he was plunging headlong toward the bottom of the
globe in search of a strait that few of the men had any
reason to believe existed. At the time, enlisted sailors, as
opposed to officers, were ostensibly regulated by a loosely
organized body of medieval maritime rules called the laws
of Rhodes and Oleron, which state that "a ship's company
are entitled to refuse to undertake a voyage that will jeop-
ardize their lives." Without a doubt, many of Magellan's
men rightly felt that in forcing them into the icy unknown
their captain-general was risking their lives.

The captains' case is more complicated. They had sworn
loyalty to the Spanish king, but their conception of their
duty was no doubt complicated by other alliances, and

from the outset they plotted and intrigued among themselves to overthrow Magellan. Although it is possible that the captains truly believed that Magellan was recklessly endangering the king's ships, it is more likely that their behavior was governed by jealousy and ambition. All three had ties of kinship or friendship to important individuals in the Spanish government who wished to wrest control of the expedition from Magellan. Indeed, the three owed their positions to these powerful allies. Furthermore, Cartagena believed that he had been given a rank equal to Magellan's, and he resented taking orders from the captain-general. Pigafetta provides another reason for the captains' disloyalty: "For the masters and captains of his other ships loved him not. I do not know the reason, unless it be that he, the captain-general, was Portuguese, and they were Spaniards or Castilians, which peoples have long borne ill-will and malevolence toward one another." Magellan was aware of the animosity toward him because of his Portuguese blood and for that reason had tried to enlist as many Portuguese as possible to man his ships, but these efforts were undercut by the savvy conspirators at the Spanish royal court.

Magellan's treatment of the rebels was as severe as his actions following their earlier defiance had been lenient. Their trial was convened ashore on April 4. In accordance with the custom of the time, the slain Mendoza was called as a defendant. Addressing himself to the bloody corpse, Magellan declared it guilty of treason and condemned it to be hanged, drawn, and quartered—the traitor's death. The quarters of the mutilated body were hung on gibbets.

Quesada was the next defendant. He was also accused of treason, and he had attacked and wounded Lloriaga. His sentence was the same as Mendoza's. This was truly a dreadful punishment, for the Spanish method of hanging did not break the victim's neck but merely left him to strangle slowly while he was drawn (the intestines pulled out through a cut in the belly) and quartered (the limbs chopped off). No one was willing to act as executioner, so Magellan offered a pardon to one of the rebels, Quesada's foster brother and secretary, Luis de Molina, if Molina would agree to kill Quesada. When Magellan said that Molina could behead Quesada with his sword, the terrified Quesada begged Molina to agree—any end was better than the traitor's death. So it was done, and the body was hoisted on another gibbet.

Having demonstrated beyond all doubt that he would tolerate no further breaches in discipline, Magellan sentenced the 45 other rebels to hard labor in chains. Cartagena owed his survival to his influential connections at court, while Elcano was spared because of his value as a pilot. (Although captains were the ranking officers aboard their ships, they were often given commands because of their connections and prestige, not necessarily because of seagoing experience or navigational expertise. A captain often relied on his pilot on points concerning navigation, although he made the final decision and bore the ultimate responsibility.) Cartagena was sentenced to house arrest in a crude wooden cabin on shore. Another instigator, a priest, Padre Pedro Sanchez de Reina, escaped the gibbet

A 1602 map of lower South America shows the "Rio Della Plata," the great river Magellan mistook for el paso. Far south, labeled "Fretum Magellanicum," is the actual strait that bears his name. The abundance of place names on the map indicates that Europeans had become much more familiar with the region in the 80 or so years since Magellan had been there, but the cartographer was still apparently willing to credit Antonio Pigafetta's reports of giant, arrow-swallowing Indians.

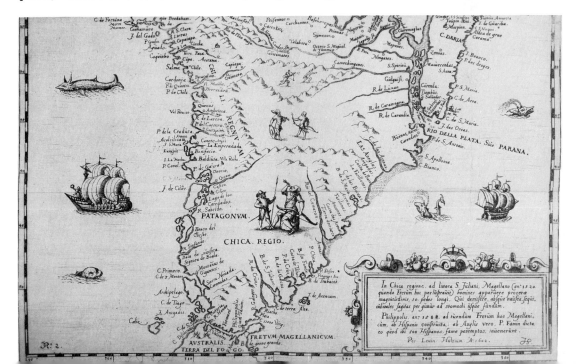

because Magellan's faith made him reluctant, for the moment, to sentence a clergyman to death.

Bad weather and hard work defined the next few months. Upon taking inventory of the ships' stores, Magellan discovered that his enemies in Spain had falsified receipts for the delivery of supplies; this meant that the fleet now had considerably less biscuit, wine, and other staples than he had believed. Loyal officers and crew were set to work gathering food. Fortunately, the seemingly desolate region proved as rich in game as Magellan had claimed and yielded to the hungry mariners shellfish, ducks, penguins (which they killed in the hundreds with clubs), and guanacos (long-necked, woolly mammals related to llamas and camels). While their shipmates hunted and scoured the cliffs and plains for firewood, the mutineers careened the ships, a difficult but necessary process that involved beaching a vessel and then shifting all its cargo and heavy guns to one side so that the ship would roll that way. In this way rotten timbers below the waterline could be dug out and replaced, leaks plugged, barnacles

As Magellan had predicted, his crew had little trouble finding food at Port San Julián. Awkward and trusting, the birds Pigafetta called black geese (penguins) were easy prey for the club-wielding mariners.

scraped, and a protective coating of hot tar spread over the hull. Captain Mesquita was put in charge of this work force. Furious at having been captured by Quesada and the other rebels, he was determined to make the manacled mutineers suffer, and Magellan ultimately had to intervene to ensure that Mesquita gave the men enough food to keep them alive while they worked.

Although his fleet was anchored at Port San Julián, Magellan's mind was still at sea, in search of *el paso*, the passage, which he believed would take him to the Spice Islands. Not realizing that by doing so he would be sailing even closer to the frigid Antarctic regions, Magellan began to consider moving the fleet southward. He sent Serrão in the *Santiago*, the smallest and most agile of the fleet's ships, to make a reconnaissance along the coast.

Serrão's sojourn soon turned into a desperate adventure. Sailing into the heart of the Antarctic winter, Serrão encountered a fearsome storm. So fierce were its winds that it took the *Santiago* 16 days to beat its way 50 miles (80 kilometers) along the coast. There, Serrão sighted the first break in the bleak coastal cliffs—an estuary, or river mouth, that he named the Santa Cruz, for he found it on May 3, which Catholics celebrate as the Feast of the Holy Cross. After a week there, Serrão and the *Santiago* once more stood out to sea to continue the reconnaissance south, but another tempest drove the little ship relentlessly away from open water, back into the shallows of the river mouth. The *Santiago*'s rudder was torn away by a huge wave, and the wind ripped out its mast. Serrão proved himself a master seaman by guiding the ship to a sandbar, where the *Santiago* held together just long enough for its crew to leap to safety; one unfortunate sailor, Serrão's slave, was caught by a wave and drowned. The pounding sea then broke up the ship and drove the remains of the wreck off the sandbar into the storm.

Serrão and his men found themselves marooned on a deserted shore, on the wrong side of a big river, in the

The guanaco is a woolly ruminant, related to the camel, that inhabits Patagonia. Pigafetta describes them as being equal parts mule, camel, stag, and horse. The guanaco also served as a food source for the sailors wintering at Port San Julián.

middle of winter, with no food and no supplies except the clothes on their backs. They managed to start a fire, and Serrão sent two volunteers to carry word to Port San Julián. They crossed the Santa Cruz River on a raft made of planks from the wrecked *Santiago* and walked north along the coast for 11 days, subsisting on shellfish and weeds, melting snow for water. When they finally stumbled into camp, they were so ragged and emaciated that their companions did not recognize them. A rescue party was sent, and the castaways were back at Port San Julián several weeks later.

In the meantime, the mariners had been diverted from the increasing harshness of the southern winter by the first outside human contact they had in several weeks. Three months earlier and more than 2,000 miles (3,200 kilometers) to the north, Magellan's men had encountered Indians, near the present-day site of Rio de Janeiro, but during their first days at Port San Julián they had seen no sign of human life. In early June, Indians began approaching the bay, and by means of gifts of mirrors, bells, and cloth the sailors were able to establish friendly relations with them; some accounts say that at least one Indian was baptized a Christian. The Indians were fascinated by the newcomers to this desolate region, as were the Spanish by the great height of the men of the tribe. But the good fellowship between the two groups was abruptly broken when Magellan clamped two towering Indian men into leg irons, hoping to take them back to King Charles in Spain. When a squad of men under the command of João Lopes Carvalho, a pilot, tried to seize several more Indians from a nearby village, a fight broke out, and one Spaniard was killed. These incidents cost Magellan the friendship of the Indians, who began to harass the intruders.

This unwelcome attention of the desolate region's native inhabitants convinced Magellan that it was time to move on. He had been impressed with Serrão's description of Santa Cruz—plenty of wood and shellfish, fresh water, a good sandy bottom to anchor in, and no Indians—and he decided to move the fleet south and await more favorable weather in this new harbor. By the latter half of the month of August, with a revamped chain of command, the fleet, now numbering four ships, was ready to sail. Only one piece of business remained: the disposition of the intransigent Cartagena and his recalcitrant crony, Padre Sanchez de Reina. The two had spent the past months attempting to foment further insurrection, and the captain-general had lost patience. When the four ships departed Port San Julián on August 24, the conspirators remained ashore, on Magellan's order, to keep company with the gibbeted remains of their fellow conspirators. Although the unyielding captain-general remained deaf to their entreaties that he allow them to accompany the fleet, he did supply them with hardtack (a hard biscuit or bread made of flour and water), wine, firearms, and gunpowder—the standard fodder and supplies of the Spanish explorer of the day. How useful these provisions proved to be remains a mystery, for the two mutineers were never seen or heard from again.

This 16th-century engraving portrays the outlandish sights and creatures that superstitious Europeans believed Magellan would encounter on his emergence from el paso into the uncharted waters of the South Sea. His actual experience, although not as fantastic, was no less extraordinary.

East and West

The Portugal in which Ferdinand Magellan was born near the close of the 15th century was Europe's farthest-ranging sea power. Isolated from the rest of the continent by rugged mountain ranges, this tiny nation tucked into the southwestern corner of the Iberian Peninsula possessed little in the way of natural resources, yet in the 60 years before Magellan's birth in or around 1480 it had taken the lead in the exploration of new sea routes and in the exploitation of the new lands to which they led.

Much of this exploration was motivated by economics. Europeans desired to reach Asia in order to exploit the trade in such alluring Eastern wares as silk, jade, gems, and especially spices, the most valuable commodity to be had from the East. To Europeans of Magellan's time, a "spice" was any of the hundreds of products that were culled or made from exotic, non-European plants: sugar, dyes, perfumes, coffee and tea, cosmetics, drugs, scented woods such as sandalwood, gums or resins such as the incense that was used in religious ceremonies, waxes, even glue. But the true spices—pepper, nutmeg, mace, cinnamon, and cloves—were the most prized of all. By the 14th century, these had become enormously popular in Europe, where, because farmers could seldom produce enough hay or oats to feed their livestock through the long northern winters, most meat animals had to be slaughtered each fall. The meat was smoked or pickled. Pepper and other seasonings helped preserve the meat—and also greatly improved its taste and that of other foods as well.

Henry the Navigator, the Portuguese prince who sponsored his nation's first great voyages of discovery. As devoted to his Catholic faith as he was to science and geography, Henry wore a hair shirt each day and maintained a lifelong celibacy.

Europeans craved the taste of spices to such an extent that it became fashionable for the wealthy to sprinkle mixed sugar and pepper on their toast.

Pepper and other spices reached European consumers by way of a long and complicated trade route. They came from what were generally called the Indies—distant Eastern lands that few Europeans had heard of and fewer still had seen. Cinnamon came from Ceylon (now known as Sri Lanka); pepper from India and from Sumatra in present-day Indonesia; nutmeg and mace from the Ambon island group in the Banda Sea, also part of present-day Indonesia; and cloves from the Spice Islands, a handful of tiny islands north of Ambon. The largest of the Spice Islands were Tidore and Ternate. These islands were also called the Moluccas, and that name gradually came to be used for all the spice-growing islands of eastern Indonesia between Borneo and New Guinea.

In large, heavy cargo ships called junks, Chinese and Malayan merchants plied the waters of the Moluccas, buying fragrant bark, berries, and leaves to sell in the port city of Malacca, a great trading center near the southern tip of the Malaysian peninsula. The cargoes that reached Malacca through the swarms of pirates that infested the Java Sea fetched good prices from Indian traders, who shipped the spices to Cochin, Calicut, Goa, and other trade ports on the Malabar Coast, as western India was then called. There Arab merchants loaded their nimble sailing vessels, called dhows, for the next leg of the trade route to Europe. Some shipments traveled across the Arabian Sea and up the Persian Gulf, to be carried by camel to Baghdad and then to markets in Beirut, Damascus, or Constantinople. Some were shipped across the Indian Ocean and up the Red Sea to Suez, then on to Cairo and Alexandria. Eventually, however, all the spices of the East came to the eastern Mediterranean, where for the first time they passed into European hands. Rich and powerful shipping families in the seafaring Italian cities of Venice and Genoa, backed by the great banking houses of central Europe, controlled the eastern Mediterranean and monopolized the spice trade. Venice, in particular, grew rich on the trade; along the Rialto, the street where the big trading companies were located, a bale of spices that had been purchased for 1 gold ducat in the Moluccas sold for 100 ducats to dealers who then distributed it to consumers all across the Continent. All the while, kings and merchants in every European nation coveted the wealth of Venice. During the 15th century, they began to dream of bypassing the Venetians and Arabs entirely—that is, of finding a new way to reach the spice-laden East. By that time, however, land routes were closed to the Christian nations of Europe by the Ottoman Turks, who controlled western Asia, and by the Ming dynasty rulers of China, who refused to allow outsiders into their country. So the Europeans turned to the sea.

A late-16th-century engraving of the city of Lisbon. While Magellan was growing up, Lisbon's mariners had made Portugal an even more powerful and prosperous nation than its neighbor on the Iberian peninsula, Spain. "If Spain is the head of Europe, Portugal, where land ends and sea begins, is the crown upon the head," wrote the 16th-century poet Luíz de Camões, author of The Lusiads, *Portugal's national epic.*

The great European age of discovery that was to produce such mariners as Columbus, Vasco da Gama, Magellan, and Sir Francis Drake began in Portugal in 1419, when a prince named Henry was made governor of the Algarve, Portugal's southwesternmost province. According to his contemporary and biographer Gomes Eanes de Zurara, at Henry's birth the stars foretold that "this prince was bound to engage in great and noble conquests, and above all he was bound to attempt the discovery of things which were hidden from other men, and secret." In the Algarve, Prince Henry the Navigator, as he came to be called, devoted himself to the study of geography. He built a small fort near the village of Sagres, on a cliff that thrust out

Venice in 1338, at the height of the prosperity its control of the spice trade and commerce with the Levant had made possible.

into the Atlantic, and he invited merchants, travelers, and sailors to visit him, eagerly making notes of their recollections of currents, winds, and coastlines. He stocked his observatory with telescopes and his library with maps and books—and he became convinced that the Indian Ocean and the lands to the east could be reached by sailing south and then east, around Africa. At Sagres was perfected the use of the quadrant, cross-staff, and compass for navigation, and it was Henry's shipbuilders who developed the first caravels—fleet, maneuverable vessels that combined the cargo-carrying capacity of the Arab dhows with the agility of Portuguese river vessels. Caravels were to prove perfectly suited to voyages of exploration. Before his death in 1460, Henry outfitted and launched a series of ocean expeditions that pushed the boundaries of the known world ever outward.

Among Prince Henry's navigators was Nuno Tristão, who in three voyages between 1441 and 1446 mapped the western bulge of Africa as far south as the mouth of the Saloum River in present-day Senegal. Henry was profoundly excited when, in 1444, one of his expeditions rounded Cape Verde, the westernmost point of Africa. Beyond Cape Verde, the great bulk of the continent fell away to the east and south, and the prince was certain that his navigators would soon sail around it entirely and emerge into the Indian Ocean. As it turned out, however, Henry had vastly underestimated the size of the African continent, and by the time of his death the farthest point reached by his expeditions was the coast of what is today Sierra Leone. Also in 1444, one of Henry's ships brought back some precious cargo—250 Africans to be sold as slaves. This demonstration of the profit to be gained from the prince's explorations quieted those who had criticized the voyages as a frivolous quest after the unknowable.

After Henry's death, the kings of Portugal continued to send out new expeditions. Each doggedly inched its way southward along the unknown west coast of Africa, battling

(continued on page 34)

Caravels made possible the first great voyages of discovery. Developed by Henry the Navigator's shipbuilders and mariners, caravels were smaller and more maneuverable than the heavy cargo ships used in the Mediterranean at the time. Their greatest asset was their ability to sail against the wind, which was provided them by the use of lateen rigging, which employed triangular sails that could be angled into the wind. Caravels used square rigging during long, open-sea passages backed by favorable wind.

Around
a Round World

Fallacies and misinterpretations sometimes become enshrined as history. Among the most enduring of these popular myths is the belief that Europeans thought the world was flat until Columbus proved that it was round by not falling off its edge on his first voyage to the New World. In fact, all educated people (and most everyone else) were well aware that the world was round long before Columbus's day.

The first people to apply science and logic to the study of the earth's shape were the ancient Greeks. Aristotle (384–322 B.C.) pointed out that the circular shadow cast by the earth upon the moon during an eclipse meant that the earth was round. A century later, the Greek philosopher Eratosthenes (ca. 276–ca.194 B.C.), working in the Egyptian city of Alexandria, calculated the distance around the earth. He arrived at a figure of 25,000 miles (40,000 kilometers), remarkably close to the actual circumference of 24,902 miles (39,843 kilometers). Later Alexandrian scholars, however, revised his calculations and came up with much smaller figures—a fact that was to have unfortunate consequences for the mariners of later generations.

Thus, although the Greeks and other ancients were often confused about the sizes and shapes of the various lands and seas that lay scattered across the earth's surface, they had a fair idea of the overall shape of that surface. It was the Christian religious philosophers of the Dark Ages who first gave credence to the notion that the earth was flat. St. Augustine (A.D. 354–430) complained that curiosity about the natural world was a sin and wrote, "What concern is it to me whether the heavens as a sphere enclose the Earth in the middle of the universe or overhang it on either side?" A 6th-century monk named Cosmas described the universe as a box, with the earth as its flat bottom and the sky as its walls. Drawing upon biblical images, these and other religious writers maintained not only that the earth was flat but that Jerusalem was its geographic center.

By the 11th century or so, Europeans had begun to be influenced by the thinking of Arab writers who had translated and preserved the works of Aristotle and Eratosthenes. European intellectuals of the 12th and 13th centuries—men like Roger Bacon, Albertus Magnus, and John of Holywood—accepted the roundness of the world as indisputable. By Columbus's time, most people correctly believed the world to be spherical; they simply underestimated its size, believing that China, Japan, and the rest of the mysterious lands described by Marco Polo and other travelers lay a short distance west across the Atlantic Ocean. Mariners such as Columbus and Magellan, who expected to reach the East by sailing west, were not challenging entrenched but mistaken beliefs with bold new geographic theories of their own—they were merely more daring and more willing to take risks than others were.

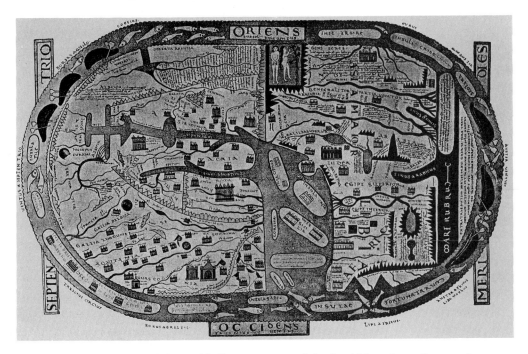

This 8th-century map of the world illustrates some of the fanciful notions of geography then prevalent.

Boabdil, the last Moorish king in Spain, surrenders the keys of the Alhambra, the Moors' palace in Granada, to Ferdinand and Isabella of Spain. Their war with the Moors over, Spain's Catholic monarchs now had the money to sponsor Columbus's proposed westward voyage to the Indies.

(continued from page 31)

heat, disease, shoal water, and, occasionally, native inhabitants. In 1473, the Portuguese crossed the equator. In 1483, Diogo Cão passed the mouth of the Congo River. The following year, an Italian navigator from Genoa, Christopher Columbus, tried to interest King João II of Portugal in a scheme to reach Asia by sailing westward across the Atlantic. (At the time, the Pacific Ocean was unknown to Europeans, as were North and South America. Columbus and others believed that Asia probably lay at some undetermined distance across the Atlantic.) But the Portuguese had spent more than half a century pioneering the eastern route around Africa, and João declined to back Columbus's venture. His decision seemed to be justified when, in 1487–88, his captain Bartolomeu Dias rounded the southern tip of the Dark Continent and entered the Indian Ocean. The pleading of his crew con-

vinced Dias to turn around and return to Portugal without reaching India, but Dias did succeed in proving that it was indeed possible to sail around Africa. The navigator called the great promontory at the bottom of the continent the Cape of Storms, but the king renamed it the Cape of Good Hope to signify his expectation that Portugal had finally found its sea route to the Indies. It would be 10 eventful years before that hope was fulfilled—years in which Magellan grew to manhood at the royal court of Portugal.

The exact date of Magellan's birth is unknown, but historians agree that it probably took place in 1480. For centuries, it was thought that his birthplace was the town of Sabrosa, in Trás-os-Montes, Portugal's northeastern province; in recent years, however, scholars studying old documents have suggested that Magellan was born in the neighboring province of Minho. Several buildings in these stony, mountainous provinces have been called "Magellan's birthplace" or "Magellan's home," but the true site is not known.

Little more is known about Magellan's family. His father was Ruy Magalhães and his mother was Alda, a daughter of the Mesquita family. Ferdinand was their third child. He had an older sister, Isabel, and an older brother, Diogo; he may also have had one or two younger sisters. The family belonged to one of the lower ranks of the Portuguese nobility, which meant that the Magellans had the privilege of sending their sons to serve as pages, or attendants, in the royal court at Lisbon. So it was to this great city, the capital and chief port of the world's foremost seafaring power, that Magellan was dispatched in 1492 to serve as a page to Queen Leonor. He and the other pages came

Pope Alexander VI, whose Treaty of Tordesillas divided the New World between Spain and Portugal. Wrote the Florentine political philosopher Niccolò Machiavelli of the Holy Father: "Of all the pontiffs who have ever reigned, [Alexander VI] best showed how a Pope might prevail both by money and force."

under the supervision of Duke Manoel, the queen's brother. Several of the 16th-century chroniclers of Magellan's life reported that the duke took an almost immediate dislike to the young Magellan, although none of them knew why. Whatever the truth of this bit of court gossip, the later relationship between the two men was an icy one.

If the boy Magellan had not heard about the voyages of Cão, Dias, and the other Portuguese mariners while he was growing up in the landlocked eastern mountains, he certainly learned of them upon his arrival at court, for training in astronomy and navigation was part of the pages' education. Furthermore, the year after Magellan came to Lisbon marked a fateful turning point in the history of exploration. In April 1493, Columbus, whose westward search for Asia had finally been sponsored by the king and queen of Spain, made his triumphant arrival at the Spanish royal court in Barcelona, where the monarchs Ferdinand and Isabella honored him for what most believed had been a voyage to the easternmost islands of the Indies.

Although it did not become clear for some years that Columbus had discovered a path to two unknown continents instead of a new route to Asia, the discovery did ignite a barrage of claims and counterclaims by Portugal and Spain. Convinced that it had already discovered the most lucrative trade route to the Indies, Portugal wanted no competition from its Iberian rival, and Spain was likewise eager to cement control over what it believed was an important new course to Asia. As all the nations of Europe were Catholic at that time, the continent's monarchs were in agreement as to the supreme spiritual sovereignty of the pope, the head of the Catholic church, and also sometimes submitted temporal questions to his holiness for mediation. The new pope, Alexander VI, who would win fame for his cunning, his dissoluteness, and his illegitimate children (the Renaissance prince Cesare Borgia and his notorious sister Lucrezia), agreed to settle the matter.

An inspired sailor but an inept administrator, Christopher Columbus was returned to Ferdinand and Isabella in chains following his third voyage to the New World. Columbus's unhappy fate foretold the treatment that several other explorers, Vasco Núñez de Balboa and Magellan among them, would receive from Spain's ungrateful monarchs.

Anxious not to alienate either nation, he essentially granted both Spain and Portugal what they wanted. By virtue of the Treaty of Tordesillas, which Alexander proclaimed in 1494, an imaginary line was drawn down the middle of the Atlantic Ocean, 370 leagues (about 2,310 miles or 3,696 kilometers) west of the Cape Verde Islands. Portugal was given the sole right to explore and to claim newly discovered lands to the east of the line, Spain to the west. The treaty thus confirmed Portugal's control of the eastern route to Asia that it had been developing for so many years and gave Spain control of its newly discovered western route.

Now that it appeared that Columbus had provided the Spanish with an opportunity to reach the Indies, the Portuguese were determined to get there first, and they possessed inside information that was sure to be useful. A Portuguese adventurer named Pero da Covilhã had spent the years 1487–90 traveling to Egypt, down the Red Sea, and across the Indian Ocean with a party of Arab traders. His landing on the Malabar Coast made him the first Portuguese to reach India. While there he visited several of the trade ports and learned much about the spice business, then crossed over to Africa and made his way from one Arab trading post to the next, finally reaching Sofala, about two-thirds of the way down the east coast of the continent. Upon his return to Cairo, he sent King João a long report full of information about harbors, winds, and sailing conditions that would prove invaluable to later explorers who entered those waters from the south. (Unfortunately for Covilhã, King João's orders next sent him to the mountain kingdom of Ethiopia, where at the insistence of the Ethiopian monarch he remained for more than 30 years, something between a prisoner and an ambassador.)

Duke Manoel became king of Portugal in 1495. He completed preparations that had begun under King João for an expedition that was to follow Dias's route around the Cape of Good Hope and then, using Covilhã's information, to go north along the coast of Africa and east to India. The Portuguese fleet, consisting of four ships led by Vasco da Gama, set off in 1497. It took 13 weeks to reach and round the Cape. This remarkable passage was conducted out of sight of land, the longest such open-sea voyage made by Europeans to that time. After nearly five more months, da Gama reached India, acquired a load of spices, and returned to Lisbon in 1499, after a long and difficult voyage home, with proof that Portugal at last had its own route to the Indies. In a letter to King Ferdinand and Queen Isabella of Spain, who had just become his in-laws, King Manoel gloated:

> We learn that they did reach and discover India and other kingdoms and lordships bordering upon it; that they entered and navigated its seas, finding large cities, large edifices and rivers, and great populations, among whom is carried on all the trade in spices and precious stones.

A detail from an official Portuguese padron, *the map of the world on which all new discoveries were recorded. At the time, such discoveries were closely guarded national secrets; a copy of this padron was smuggled from Portugal in 1502 by Alberto Cantino, a spy in the employ of the Duke of Ferrara. Reflecting Portugal's commercial interests, the mapmaker was apparently very familiar with the Mediterranean world and Africa's west coast, much less so with northern Europe.*

In its immediate ramifications, da Gama's expedition was more momentous than Columbus's discovery. The Genoan believed he had reached the Indies, but as yet his voyage had borne no great economic benefit for Spain, which was to this point still unaware that what Columbus had drifted upon was essentially the gateway to two great continents. Da Gama's voyage, by contrast, had delivered to Portugal what Columbus had promised to provide Ferdinand and Isabella: a route to the Indies that would enable his nation to play a direct role in the spice trade. Its effects were almost instantaneous. By 1503 pepper sold in Lisbon for one-fifth of what it cost in Venice, and over the ensuing decades, power in Europe would shift from those states that dominated the Mediterranean to those that controlled the oceans.

Magellan was 19 years old when da Gama returned from India. His apprenticeship as a page was over; he now had the rank of squire and since 1496 had been a clerk in the Casa da India, the government bureau that organized maritime expeditions and controlled the Eastern trade. He may even have helped keep records or buy supplies for da Gama's expedition. Also working in the Casa da India was a young man named Francisco Serrão, who some historians believe was a distant cousin of Magellan's. Whether or not the two were related, they became fast friends. It was a friendship that was to help shape Magellan's destiny.

With the sea road to India now open, Portugal lost no time in sending out new armadas to reap the wealth of the East. One fleet, under the command of Pedro Álvars Cabral, while swinging west of da Gama's course in the Atlantic, unexpectedly came upon what is now known as Brazil. Cabral established that this new (to Europeans) region extended east past the pope's line of demarcation and therefore belonged to Portugal, although the Portuguese made no serious attempt to exploit this find until the 1530s. After Cabral's voyage, Manoel sent some secret expeditions westward to the Americas to examine Spain's

This portrait of Vasco da Gama, the Portuguese mariner who discovered the sea route to the Indies, originally hung in the Portuguese royal palace in Goa, the capital of Portuguese India. In its immediate ramifications, da Gama's voyage was even more momentous than Columbus's.

half of the world; the reports of these missions were closely guarded in the Casa da India, but Magellan may well have seen or heard of them. The real thrust of Portugal's activity, however, was eastward. Overnight, it seemed, this barren little country on the fringe of Europe displaced Venice as the center of the spice trade and grew astonishingly rich. The Arabs, who had controlled the Indian Ocean trade for centuries, were not going to surrender their monopoly without a fight. They attacked Portuguese ships and conspired to turn the rajahs and princes who controlled the ports of the Malabar Coast against the Europeans.

By 1505, King Manoel had enough of this interference. He sent a 22-ship military fleet under Francisco de Almeida to quell the Arabs and their allies, the African and Indian Muslims, along the east coast of Africa and the west coast of India. The 25-year-old Magellan received the king's permission to enlist in the expedition.

A detail from an ornately illustrated Portuguese padron of 1519, showing the horn of Africa, the Arabian Peninsula, and the Indian subcontinent. Clearly impressed by the accounts given by Portuguese voyagers to the East, the cartographer has included beautiful depictions of the region's architecture, flora and fauna, and inhabitants.

C: de Gel

A Soldier of Portugal

Along with Francisco Serrão, Magellan signed on with Almeida as a *sobresaliente*, or gentleman-adventurer without pay. Unlike the common seamen, they had no duties to perform, but they enjoyed no greater comforts. They slept on the crowded deck and ate moldy biscuit and rotting salt pork and beef like everyone else did. It is not known which ship they sailed on, but it may have been the one that was captained by João Serrão, who was either Francisco's older brother or his cousin. João Serrão's future was to be even more closely intertwined with Magellan's than was Francisco's.

After a rough voyage through frigid, stormy waters far to the south, the fleet rounded the Cape of Good Hope, then proceeded up the African coast, sacking and burning Arab trading posts and massacring the inhabitants as it went. The fighting was especially brutal because Christians and Muslims each regarded the other as infidels, heathens to whom the obligations and courtesies owed a fellow believer did not apply. Before long, the Portuguese controlled such important centers of trade on Africa's east coast as Kilwa and Mombasa. During this period, a captain named Nuno Pereira appointed Magellan to the post of pilot's assistant on a barge that was equipped with cannons to blow up Arab shippers and smugglers in coastal waters. In 15 months, Magellan sank more than 200 Arab dhows and learned a great deal about inshore seamanship on unfamiliar coasts.

A late-16th-century engraving by Theodore de Bry of a Portuguese armada departing Lisbon. The ships depicted, with their three masts and high stern castles and forecastles, were probably very similar to the ones on which Magellan traveled to India.

Harvesters reap pepper in the Moluccas in this 1537 woodcut. Like most Europeans, the artist was unfamiliar with pepper in its native habitat. Piper nigrum *(black pepper) is a climbing shrub, not a tree; the spice is culled from pea-sized berries that it bears.*

When Pereira was transferred to the Malabar Coast in 1507, he took Magellan with him. Skirmishing between the Arabs and the Portuguese continued, with neither side able to gain the upper hand, but when Almeida's son was killed in an attack on the port of Dabul in 1509, the war escalated. Almeida mustered every Portuguese ship in the Indian Ocean, sailed on Dabul, and burned the town to the ground, slaughtering every man, woman, and child within its walls. Egyptians and Venetians who had joined forces with the Arabs to protect their interests in the spice trade were among the victims of Almeida's merciless revenge. Almeida then tracked the Arab fleet—200 large dhows and about 20,000 men—to the island of Diu. With only 19 ships and 1,800 men, Almeida nonetheless launched a furious attack. The Portuguese succeeded in wiping out about half of the Arab force, but their own losses were heavy. Among the dead was Pereira, and Magellan was so gravely wounded that he was not expected to survive. However, after five months in a hospital in the Malabar trading port of Cochin, which had earlier been captured by the Portuguese, Magellan was fit to rejoin the fleet.

Victories on the African and Indian coasts did not satisfy the Portuguese, who wanted to secure a firm grip on the spice trade before Spain managed to reach the East. To do so, Portugal would have to get closer to the Spice Islands themselves, which lay an unknown distance east of India. Almeida decided to eliminate the Malayan middlemen in the spice trade by capturing Malacca, the great trade center on the Malaysian waterway that controlled access to the Moluccas. He sent five ships under the command of Diogo Lopes de Sequeira to establish Portuguese control there. Magellan and his friend Francisco Serrão were part of this expedition.

The Portuguese who reached Malacca in September 1509 found a large, cosmopolitan city ruled by a Muslim sultan. Commerce was the city's lifeblood. Vessels from

China, Arabia, India, Ceylon, and the Spice Islands thronged its harbor, and the streets and marketplaces were lined with warehouses and trading stations. The sultan was none too pleased to see five heavily armed foreign ships in his harbor, but warned by his Arab counselors of the damage that Portuguese guns could do, he greeted the newcomers with a show of friendship. Sequeira's men were given the run of the city, and as they hurried ashore to enjoy themselves and to barter for fortunes of their own, a local chief visited the flagship to play chess with Sequeira. Although all seemed serene, Serrão mistrusted the sultan, and he warned Sequeira to beware of treachery. Sequeira

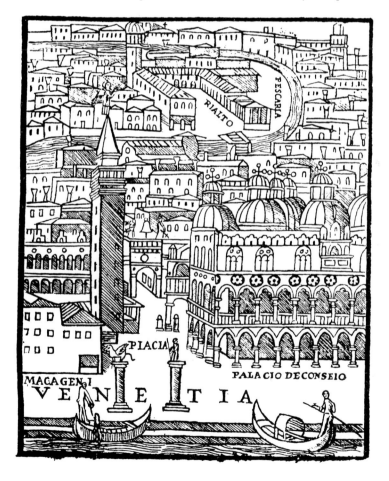

A 1517 woodcut of Venice. The city of canals had already entered its period of decline, owing, in large part, to Portugal's discovery of a trade route to the Indies. The Rialto, home to the warehouses and offices of the great mercantile concerns, is at top.

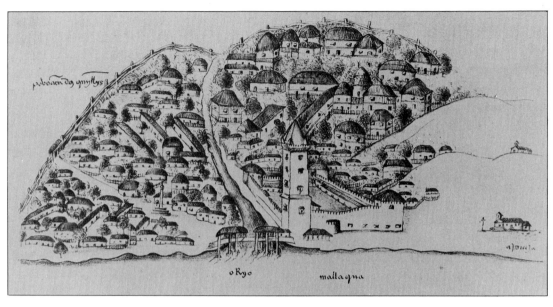

The great Muslim trading center of Malacca, on the Malaysian peninsula, fell to the Portuguese in 1511. Magellan distinguished himself in the attack and afterward most likely served as a military commander there. This engraving of Malacca is by the Portuguese artist Gaspar Correia and dates from the middle of the 15th century.

carelessly dismissed the warning, but Serrão's unease was communicated to Magellan.

Serrão's suspicions proved well founded. While blandly promising Sequeira that he would soon be able to fill the holds of his ships with pepper and cloves, the sultan had ordered troops from the interior of the country brought up in the hope of smashing the Portuguese in a surprise attack. The failure of this plan was largely attributable to the vigilant Magellan, who remained on his ship while most of the crew and officers went ashore. A captain named Garcia de Sousa noticed that a great many *praus*, the canoelike Malayan boats, seemed to be clustering around the Portuguese ships and that a large number of Malays, all armed with sharp knives, suddenly wished to come aboard for a visit and a chat. He sent Magellan to interrupt Sequeira's chess game. In an offhand tone of voice, Magellan calmly told Sequeira in Portuguese what was happening. The Portuguese commander then spoiled the sultan's surprise by driving the ambushers from his ship. Things did not go so well for the men ashore; at a signal, Malays fell upon them and began butchering them. Forty of the Portuguese, including Francisco Serrão, managed to fight off the initial onslaught and make their way onto a pier. While Magellan jumped into a small boat and rowed into the heart of the melee to save Serrão and some of the others, Sequeira was able to get his fleet safely out of the harbor. About 60 of Sequeira's men were killed or captured in the attack, but without Magellan's coolness and presence of mind, things might have gone much worse for the Portuguese.

On the return voyage to India, Magellan again saved Serrão's life. Their ship was attacked by Chinese pirates. The Portuguese managed to drive off the bandits, but Serrão and a few others were accidentally left on the Chinese junk. Accompanied by four brave seamen, Magellan rowed a small boat to the junk, boarded it, and attacked the pirates. His ferocity was such that he not only rescued his friend but captured the junk, whose hold was full of valuable spices and silks, of which Magellan received a generous share.

Meanwhile, Almeida had been replaced as viceroy of Portuguese India by Afonso de Albuquerque. When Sequeira's fleet returned from its failed mission to Malacca, Albuquerque rewarded Magellan and Serrão for their courage by making each of them captain of his own ship. Magellan then took part in the Portuguese attack on the Muslim trade port of Calicut, which turned into a disastrous defeat for the Portuguese. There Magellan suffered a second wound, and soon after he decided to return to Portugal. His share of five years' worth of loot and plunder amounted to a sizable hoard of pepper, which he could turn into a tidy fortune in Lisbon. When three ships set out for home in 1510, Magellan and his pepper were aboard one of them. Unfortunately for Magellan, the captain of his vessel was not an adept mariner, and his ship, along with another, ran aground on a reef in the Indian Ocean. The passengers and crew made it safely to a nearby island, where it was decided that the officers and noblemen of the party would take the ship's boats and row back to Cochin, about a week away, to get help. The ordinary seamen would have to stay on the barren island, as there was no room for them in the boats. Fearing that the aristocrats would not bother to come back for them, the seamen threatened to destroy the boats rather than let them leave. As a pledge of good faith, Magellan volunteered to remain with the men on the island; reassured by this, the men allowed the boats to depart.

Magellan's 16th- and 17th-century biographers devoted much attention to this incident. They felt that it demonstrated a nobility of character that enabled Magellan to relate equally well with aristocrats and commoners, but the incident also demonstrates Magellan's hardheaded practicality, for it was his self-sacrificing deed that allowed the boats to be safely launched. Had he not acted, perhaps none of the shipwreck victims, nobles or commoners, would have been rescued. He and the men endured three weeks of suspense until a rescue ship arrived. Ivory and porcelain treasures were salvaged from the wrecked ships, but Magellan's fortune—sacks of pepper—was ruined by salt water. Instead of returning home, as he originally intended, he went back to India to make another try at accumulating riches.

During this stint in the India service, Magellan commanded a warship in one of the bloodiest battles in the history of European adventures in Asia. The Muslim trading city of Goa on the southern Malabar Coast had stoutly resisted Portugal's advances in that region until, in November 1510, Albuquerque stormed the city with his fleet and put more than 8,000 men, women, and children to the sword in a single afternoon. One of Magellan's modern biographers, Ian Cameron, believes that the sack of Goa was a moral crisis for Magellan. In his book *Magellan and the First Circumnavigation of the World*, Cameron points out that an extraordinary amount of loot was plundered from Goa—so much that even the lowest-ranking soldiers received two years' pay as their share. Yet Magellan received nothing, leading Cameron to speculate that Magellan was denied a share of the plunder because he refused to take part in the massacre. But whether Magellan participated in the slaughter or not, the effect of the battle was decisive. Goa became the center of Portuguese influence on the Malabar Coast (it remained under Portugal's control until 1961), and Albuquerque, having tightened his grip on India, looked eastward to Malacca and decided that it was time to teach that city's devious sultan a lesson.

A fleet of 19 Portuguese ships, 1 of them commanded by Magellan, arrived at Malacca in July 1511. Magellan

A battle at Gujarat, north of Bombay in India, between the Portuguese and the Arabs, who were determined to protect their trade monopoly in the region. Magellan distinguished himself in many such encounters.

noticed that the city's defenses had been made considerably stronger since the last visit of the Portuguese; but although it was now protected by 3,000 cannons and 20,000 soldiers, Malacca still could not hold out against the guns of Albuquerque's ships. The city fell on August 10. Magellan's share of the plunder included a 13-year-old Malay slave boy, whom he named Henrique. From that time on, Henrique accompanied Magellan in his travels. All indications are that Magellan treated Henrique with great kindness, and Henrique clearly felt loyalty and even affection toward his master for as long as Magellan lived.

It is almost certain that Magellan remained in Malacca as one of the city's new military commanders until the end of 1511, but the trail of his activities in 1512 is blurred and hard to follow. Because it is not known exactly what he did during this mysterious year, it is impossible to say with certainty whether Magellan was really the first man to travel around the world. One theory about Magellan's whereabouts in 1512 rests on a document in the court archives of Portugal, a receipt that indicates that Magellan's monthly stipend, his salary as a member of the court, was paid out to him in Lisbon in June 1512. If the signature on that yellowed receipt is authentic, Magellan must have gone straight home to Portugal at the end of 1511 or very early in 1512 in order to have reached Lisbon by June.

Another theory holds the receipt to be a forgery and places Magellan in the Moluccas during 1512. It is known that in late 1511 Albuquerque dispatched three ships from Malacca with instructions to locate the Spice Islands. António de Abreu commanded the expedition and captained one ship; Francisco Serrão captained another. Most chroniclers say that the third ship was captained by Simon Affonso, but a 17th-century historian named Leonardo Lupercio de Argensola wrote that Magellan was the captain of the third vessel. If so, Magellan accompanied Abreu's fleet to the Ambon and Banda island groups in the Banda Sea. Having filled his hold with cloves, Abreu turned back

Afonso de Albuquerque succeeded Francisco de Almeida as Portugal's viceroy in India. Magellan served under both. An implacable enemy of the Muslims, Albuquerque took Malacca and Goa, but his greatest ambition—to steal the corpse of Muhammad, the sacred prophet of Islam, and hold it in ransom for Muslim withdrawal from the Holy Land—went unfulfilled.

to Malacca, as did Affonso (or Magellan), but Serrão's adventures were just beginning. Apparently unwilling to turn back until he had reached the Moluccas, Serrão eventually made his way to Ternate, where he set himself up as an adviser to the sultan, who was at war with his neighbor, the sultan of the neighboring island of Tidore. Over the next few years, Serrão acquired a palace, a harem, and a fair amount of power and wealth. Quite happy in his tropical paradise, he never left the Moluccas, but he did send letters to Portuguese India by native messengers. Magellan was the recipient of at least one, which informed

Never a favorite at the Portuguese royal court, the young Magellan owed the success of his early career to his prowess as a mariner and warrior. In the Portugal of the day, however, ferocity and ambition, without influential connections, could take a man only so far.

him that "I have found a New World, richer, greater and more beautiful than that of Vasco da Gama. . . . I beg you to join me here, that you may sample for yourself the delights which surround me." Despite Argensola's assertion, it seems unlikely that Magellan accompanied Abreu, but if he did, Serrão's letters make it clear that he did not reach the Moluccas.

In recent years, scholars have uncovered archival documents that suggest a third theory about Magellan's mysterious year. This thesis holds that Magellan struck out on his own on a secret and unofficial voyage of exploration, possibly in the pay of an Italian merchant named Gianno da Empoli. Certain old accounts claim that Magellan sailed across "seas no Christian man had yet entered into" and discovered a great net of islands "600 leagues northeast of Malacca." If the theory that credits Magellan with this surreptitious voyage is correct, the islands he discovered in 1512 were the Philippines.

The importance of Magellan's missing year is this: If he did sail east either to Ambon in the Banda Sea or to the southern edge of the Philippines, then he was truly the first to circumnavigate—that is, to travel completely around—the world. Either of these voyages would have carried him farther east than the farthest point west that he was to reach on the great voyage of 1519–22. If his farthest-east and farthest-west journeys overlapped in this fashion, then he did span the globe (although not in a single continuous voyage). But if he neither accompanied Abreu to Ambon nor sailed on his own to the Philippines in 1512, then he did not truly circumnavigate the world, and his claim to a place in history is simply that of a remarkable navigator, a masterful and fearless leader of men, and a bold adventurer who launched, although he did not complete, the greatest journey of all time.

The mystery of Magellan's whereabouts in 1512 may never be solved, and it is still not clear why he returned abruptly to Portugal in 1513, at the age of 33. If he had indeed made an unauthorized trip to the Philippines, it is possible that Portuguese officials in India learned of it and sent him home to get him out of the way. Ian Cameron believes that Magellan was packed off to Portugal in disgrace because he suggested that if the line of demarcation established by the Treaty of Tordesillas were extended around the world, the Spice Islands would be found to lie in the Spanish section of the world rather than in the Portuguese. Although this idea clearly guided Magellan's later actions, it is by no means certain that he expressed it as early as 1512. Perhaps he returned to Portugal simply because he was tired of the East and wanted to go home for a while. Whatever the reason, return he did, but it was to be a disappointing homecoming.

DE O IN CELO TIB AVTEN IN MVNDO

Kings and Conspiracies

Magellan arrived in Portugal sometime in 1512 or early 1513. In the few years he had been gone, the harbors at Lisbon and Oporto had grown almost beyond recognition to accommodate the burgeoning spice trade from the Indies and the commerce in slaves from the Ivory Coast of Africa. His years of service in the East had brought Magellan a slight promotion in court rank, from squire to *fidalgo escudeiro*, or gentleman in waiting, and a small increase in his monthly stipend, but Magellan appears to have been dissatisfied. No one knows just what his hopes and plans were, but he did make several requests to King Manoel: one for another promotion, one to be reassigned to service in the East, and one to be given command of his own expedition to the Moluccas. All were refused.

In 1513 a frustrated Magellan enlisted for military service in Portugal's ongoing war against the Moors, as the Islamic warriors from North Africa who conquered Spain in the 8th century were known. Some historians believe that Magellan hoped by distinguished service in Morocco to win the favorable attention of the king. Through the friendly influence of the army's transport officer, a well-known navigator called João of Lisbon, Magellan was made a *quadrilheiro mor*, an official in charge of captured prisoners and loot. Although this post was considered a desirable one because of the opportunity for profit it offered, it resulted in trouble for Magellan, probably as a

King Manoel I of Portugal. Manoel was called "the Fortunate" because he inherited so many grand enterprises upon his accession to the throne in 1495. Among these was a plan to follow up Dias's voyage around the Cape of Good Hope with a trade expedition to India.

result of jealousy on the part of rivals who had been over-looked for the potentially lucrative position. Sometime after the Battle of Azamor, in which he received the leg wound that left him lame for the rest of his life, Magellan was accused of selling captured horses back to the Moors for his own profit. His commanding officer ordered a court-martial, but Magellan returned to Lisbon in disgust without waiting for his trial or for a formal discharge from the army. He sought an audience with King Manoel, presumably to clear himself of the charges that had been made against him in Morocco, but during the interview, Magellan had the audacity to ask the king to increase his monthly stipend. Manoel refused angrily and ordered Magellan to return to Morocco to answer the charges of misconduct. Now that his enemies had succeeded in getting Magellan in trouble with the king, they were willing to let the matter drop, but with characteristic stubbornness, Magellan insisted on a full court-martial, running the risk that he might be found guilty and imprisoned. He offered his undeniable poverty as proof that he was innocent, and the charges were dismissed as "not proven."

Now discharged, Magellan returned once more to Lisbon and again sought an interview with Manoel. Eventually the audience was granted, sometime between late 1514 and 1516. Many accounts of the meeting have survived, and they agree that the outcome was a total rejection of Magellan by his king. Magellan asked for a raise in pay. He was turned down. He then asked to be assigned to service in the royal navy, probably hoping to be sent back to the Indies. He was turned down more bluntly than he had been before, Manoel's words and tone indicating that Magellan had no hope of a worthwhile post in his service. At that point, Magellan asked whether Manoel would allow him to seek service elsewhere. The king replied that Magellan could do as he pleased. As Magellan withdrew, he made to kiss the king's hand in the usual gesture of loyalty, but Manoel snatched his hand away at the last moment. The insult was complete; the bond between the nobleman and his sworn king was shattered. Magellan left the court and settled into humble quarters in the coastal city of Oporto. After two decades of loyal service and grievous injuries sustained fighting his country's wars, Ferdinand Magellan was a man without a master. He was also poor, unpopular, and out of work, but like another master mariner before him, Christopher Columbus, who also endured much hard times before achieving success, Magellan was possessed of a driving ambition and an idea that he firmly believed was worth a fortune.

The ambition was to reach the Spice Islands, from which Francisco Serrão continued to send alluring letters. The idea was that he could reach the Moluccas via a new route: by sailing west, not east. No one is quite certain of exactly when this thought took hold of Magellan, but a

Spanish conquistador Vasco Núñez de Balboa, the first European to lay eyes on the Pacific Ocean. Balboa's political instincts were less sure than was his geographical sense, and he was eventually beheaded for treason.

letter he wrote to Serrão in 1514 or 1515 hinted that it had already occurred to him. "I will come to you soon," Magellan assured his old friend, "if not by way of Portugal, then by way of Spain"; that is, by voyaging to the west, through Spanish waters. Magellan's ambiguous missive might also indicate that he was already thinking of switching his allegiance from Portugal to its old rival, Spain.

By this point, Europeans were becoming aware that the islands and shores Columbus had discovered were not the Indies but a completely new land—one, moreover, that under the terms of the Treaty of Tordesillas belonged almost entirely to Spain. But sometime in 1514, word reached Portugal of a Spanish discovery in this new world that changed people's conception of the world forever.

The discoverer was Vasco Núñez de Balboa, surely one of the most unlucky of the great Spanish conquistadors.

Three centuries later, Balboa's feat still exerted a hold on the European imagination, as evidenced by this highly romanticized early-19th-century version of the moments leading up to that instant, in poet John Keats's words, "when with eagle eyes/He stared at the Pacific—and all his men/Looked at each other with a wild surmise/Silent, upon a peak in Darién."

He was born in 1475, and in 1501 he shipped out to the Caribbean, where he settled on Hispaniola, the island that was Columbus's first major discovery in the Americas and that now is occupied by the nations of Haiti and the Dominican Republic. Balboa intended to be a farmer, but he was so unsuccessful at it that in 1510 he was forced to escape from his creditors by hiding in a barrel. The barrel was part of an expedition to what is today the Isthmus of Panama (an isthmus is a narrow strip of land that links two larger land masses and separates two bodies of water). This expedition resulted in the founding of Spain's first permanent colony on the American mainland, in the Darién region of Panama, later called the Spanish Main. Balboa, the failed farmer, soon established himself as one of the bravest and most tireless of the colonists, who rewarded him by electing him governor. Unfortunately, the settlers' mandate was never ratified by the royal government in Spain, which dispatched its own man for the post. The angered colonists refused to accept the new governor. Led by Balboa, they drove him from the colony and back to Spain.

Balboa explored Darién and questioned the natives about the area. Based on what they told him, he became convinced that an unknown sea, perhaps the sea in which the isles of the Indies would at last be found, lay not far away to the west. At the head of an expedition of about 1,000 men (mostly Indians), Balboa pushed westward through the tropical jungles of the isthmus, traversing knife-sharp ridges and steep ravines, for nearly a month. Finally, in late September 1513, from the crest of a hill, he stared at the Pacific Ocean for the first time (a moment that was later immortalized by the English poet John Keats in his sonnet "On First Looking into Chapman's Homer," although Keats mistakenly credited the discovery to "stout Cortez"). Balboa named this great body of water the South Sea and claimed it in the name of King Ferdinand of Spain.

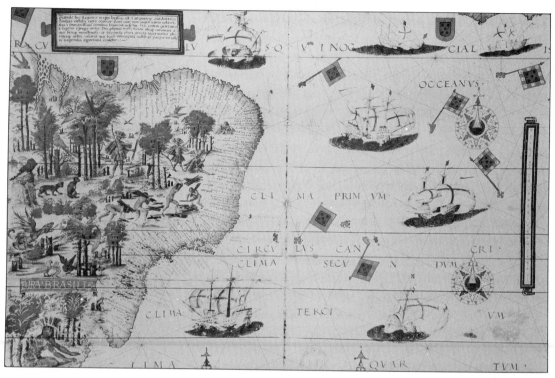

A detail from a 1519 Portuguese padron depicts the plant, animal, and human life to be found in Brazil, which the explorer Pedro Álvars Cabral claimed for Portugal in 1500. Prior to Cabral's voyage, Spain had believed that it had an exclusive claim to the New World, but Brazil proved to be to the east, or Portuguese, side of the line established by the Treaty of Tordesillas.

Balboa did not bask for long in the fame of his momentous discovery. Ferdinand made him admiral of the South Sea and of Panama, but a scheming rival for the governorship, Pedro Arias Dávila, managed to have the discoverer tried and convicted on charges of treason relating to his opposition to the earlier governor. Balboa was beheaded in January 1519, his severed head impaled on spikes in Darién.

When news of the discovery of the South Sea reached the navigators and mapmakers of Europe, most agreed with Balboa that the Indies lay on the far side of this new ocean, perhaps only a few days' sail away. Although King Ferdinand immediately ordered his followers in Panama to begin building a fleet of ships on the shore of the Pacific, he and everyone else knew that launching an expedition from there would be a long, difficult, and costly process. If only it were possible to sail from the Atlantic into the newly discovered South Sea, it might indeed be possible to reach the Indies by sailing west, just as Columbus had hoped to do. The search was on for a strait or sea passage—el paso—through the inconveniently placed Americas. Sometime in the year or two following his abrupt dismissal from King Manoel's service, Magellan became convinced that he knew where the strait would be found.

Magellan's conviction was based on his piecing together bits of geographic lore picked up during his clerkship in the Casa da India and from João of Lisbon and other navigator friends; he may even have returned to the Casa da India during 1515 or 1516 to pore over old reports. He knew that, following Cabral's discovery of Brazil, Manoel had sent João da Nova and four ships to explore the Brazilian coast in 1501. (One of the ships was captained by Diogo Barbosa, a Portuguese who later switched his allegiance to Spain. The Barbosa family was to play an important role in Magellan's future.) At that time, King Manoel maintained a cordial relationship with the Fuggers, a wealthy and powerful Austrian banking family that had controlled the distribution of spices from Venice and later from Lisbon. The Fuggers' agent in Lisbon, Cristóbal de Haro, received Manoel's permission to send three ships, under the command of Cristóbal Jacques, to scout the coast of Brazil, also in 1501. That same year, Manoel sent out yet another scouting party, this time to seek a westward strait in northern Brazil. The Italian Amerigo Vespucci was one of the officers in this fleet; he was one of the first to report that South America was a continent, not just a large island, and in his honor a German mapmaker gave the name "America" to the continent.

Haro, the Fuggers' agent, sent two more expeditions to Brazil in 1503. One was led by Gonzalo Coelho, the other by Jacques, who rounded the bulge of Brazil and headed south along the coast of the continent, in the process crossing over the treaty line into Spain's territory. In what is now Argentina, Jacques discovered a wide, deep-water

In this 1586 engraving, Amerigo Vespucci uses an unlikely looking astrolabe to chart the position of the Southern Cross. From a prominent Florentine family, Vespucci was sailing for Manoel I of Portugal when he made the voyage in 1501 that proved South America was a continent. It is noteworthy that the engraver has given his subject a somewhat otherworldly air; many Europeans regarded the study of the stars as akin to wizardry.

passage into the mainland. He sailed up this passage for several days before being blown back out to sea by a storm, then returned to Portugal to report that he had found a strait. A wary Manoel ordered the report suppressed because he did not want the Spanish to learn about this supposed waterway to the Indies that lay in their own territory.

After 1510, the Fuggers and Manoel had a falling out over the division of profits from the spice trade. Haro began quietly preparing to leave Portugal, perhaps for Spain. He intended to take some valuable trade secrets with him, so in 1514 he sent João of Lisbon on a surreptitious expedition to rediscover the strait that Jacques had found a decade earlier. The Portuguese mariner located the water passage but could not linger to explore it because Haro had ordered him not to get caught sneaking around in Spanish waters. After making a hasty and rather inaccurate note of its location, he returned to Lisbon. It is known that João later visited his friend Magellan in Oporto, and it is likely that he told Magellan about this discovery. A number of historians claim that João even arranged for Magellan to visit the royal map room in Lisbon, where he would have seen the famous globe made in 1506 by the German mapmaker Martin Behaim. The Behaim globe showed a strait through South America right where Jacques and João said it was.

During this period, Magellan began spending time with an eccentric astronomer named Ruy Faleiro, who also was living in Oporto in exile from the court. Faleiro was a nervous, suspicious, and unstable man who eventually proved to be insane, but he knew something of navigational theories. He convinced Magellan that he possessed a secret technique for pinpointing a location at sea that would revolutionize navigation. Together, the two men formed something of a partnership. Magellan believed he knew where to find the westward strait through the Americas; Faleiro thought he knew how to make navigation an exact science. What they lacked was someone willing to sponsor an expedition that would allow them to prove their theories.

The strait, if it existed, lay in Spanish territorial waters, so it was natural for Magellan's thoughts to turn to Spain. A number of Portuguese who were disaffected with Manoel for one reason or another transferred their loyalty to Spain at about this time. One was the navigator Juan Díaz de Solís, who led a Spanish expedition in search of el paso. He found the passage described by Jacques and João of Lisbon but was killed by Indians before he could explore it. Another was João Serrão, one of the original captains of the Almeida armada and the relative of Magellan's friend Francisco. A third was Diogo Barbosa, a veteran of the da Nova expedition to Brazil, who had been living in Spain since 1503. He and his son Duarte, who also had sailed with Almeida, invited Magellan to join them in Seville and seek his fortune in service to Charles I, the new king of Spain. When the Barbosas promised to use their influence to get Magellan the command of an expedition to seek el paso, he hesitated no longer. In October 1517, he crossed the mountains from his homeland into Spain.

Magellan and Henrique took up residence in the Barbosa household. Several months later, Magellan married Diogo Barbosa's daughter Beatriz, but he had little time to enjoy the pleasures of domestic life, for he immediately found himself caught up in a tangle of court intrigue. Winning an expedition from King Charles, he soon learned, would not be as easy as he had hoped. Simply getting the king's ear proved quite difficult.

The Barbosas had counted on their plan gaining the support of Juan de Fonseca, the bishop of Burgos, who was one of the young king's most influential advisers, but Cristóbal de Haro, who had fled to Spain late in 1516 after King Manoel high-handedly confiscated several Fugger cargoes, had made Fonseca a partner in a scheme of

Charles I of Spain at age 18, two years after he assumed the Spanish throne in 1516. In Charles's first years on the throne, few had great hopes for his reign. A member of the Hapsburg family of Austria, he spoke no Spanish, but under his rule Spain found itself the possessor of a vast colonial empire, much of it in the Americas.

After being rejected by Manoel, an embittered Magellan, who had been wounded several times while in the service of his king, took his plans for an expedition to the Indies to King Charles of Spain.

his own. Haro wanted one of the Fugger pilots, Estevão Gomes, to lead the expedition to the strait, and to get Fonseca's support he suggested to the bishop that Juan de Cartagena could share the command. Cartagena was Fonseca's heir; he was politely referred to as the bishop's nephew, but he was really an illegitimate son. Fonseca and Haro agreed to combine forces to oppose the Barbosa-Magellan expedition in favor of a Gomes-Cartagena one.

In the meantime, Magellan managed to obtain a hearing in front of the board of examiners of Spain's maritime and colonial bureau, the Casa de Antillas (sometimes called the Casa de Contratación), which had to approve all expeditions. Because he had promised Faleiro that he would not reveal the existence of the strait, Magellan did not answer the board's questions fully, and his petition was denied. But the board's chairman, Juan de Aranda, guessed what Magellan was hiding, privately persuaded him to admit the existence of the strait, and then offered to get Magellan an audience before the king's council—which had the power to overturn the decision of the Casa de Antillas—in return for a one-eighth share of the profits from the voyage. Magellan agreed (Faleiro, when he learned of this, was enraged), and Aranda arranged for them all to travel to the city of Valladolid, where the 18-year-old king was holding court. At about the same time, Fonseca and Haro were experiencing setbacks. They had presented their plan for a Gomes-Cartagena expedition to King Charles, but the young monarch had just arranged for his older sister Eleanor to marry the widowed King Manoel of Portugal. Charles feared—quite rightly—that Manoel would bitterly resent any attempt on the part of Spain to encroach on the spice trade, and he did not want to make trouble. He turned Fonseca and Haro down, but Aranda persuaded him to listen to Magellan and Faleiro. Not wanting to miss out on the chance to profit from anything that happened at court, the scheming Fonseca then threw his support behind Magellan.

Magellan and Faleiro shrewdly based their proposal to the king not on the wealth that was to be snatched from Portuguese hands but on geography. They convinced Charles that the Spice Islands lay on Spain's side of the Treaty of Tordesillas line, not on Portugal's, and that it was therefore well within Spain's rights to travel to those lands through Spanish waters. This time, King Charles gave not only his permission but also his enthusiastic support. (Ultimately, he contributed a set of 74 detailed but not very practical instructions designed to cover every circumstance of shipboard life.)

On March 22, 1518, the king, Magellan, and Faleiro signed an agreement that granted five ships and the necessary funds to the expedition. Under the terms of the contract, Magellan and Faleiro would be made governors of any islands they discovered and would be granted possession of any two islands they discovered after the first six. Together they would receive one-fifth of the profits from the voyage, to dispose of as they saw fit; the rest would belong to the crown. The goal of the expedition—to find a passage westward to the Spice Islands through a strait in South America—was not publicly announced; crewmen were asked only to sign on for two years and told that their destination would be revealed when the fleet was safely at sea. Pigafetta explains that Magellan "did not wholly declare the voyage which he wished to make, lest the people from astonishment and fear refuse to accompany him on so long a voyage as he had in mind to undertake, in view of the great and violent storms of the Ocean Sea whither he would go." Nevertheless, many people in the courts of Spain and Portugal knew what was planned, and by the time the fleet actually sailed its destination was an open secret.

Originally, Magellan and Faleiro were to be joint commanders and equal partners, but Faleiro's mental instability and general incompetence caused King Charles to order him out of the expedition shortly before it sailed, much to Magellan's relief. The navigational secret that Faleiro had promised turned out to be useless mumbo jumbo, and the irascible astronomer faded from the picture. He died in Spain in 1544, after stints in a jail and a madhouse.

Faleiro was the least of Magellan's problems. The captain-general was plagued by Portuguese agents who, on Manoel's orders, did everything they could to delay or sabotage the preparation of the fleet. It was largely the result of their bribes that Magellan was victimized by many of his suppliers and therefore set out with far fewer provisions than he had ordered. Nor did he have smooth relations with the Spanish. As soon as the expedition was announced, Fonseca and Haro began scheming to place their own representatives in important positions in the fleet. They complained to the Casa de Antillas that Magellan was hiring too many Portuguese seamen, who might prove disloyal to Spain, and the king finally had to intervene to give Magellan permission to hire 37 Portuguese. The final crew consisted of 275 or 277 men, among them Greeks, Germans, Italians, Frenchmen, Basques, Malays, Africans, Dutchmen, and one Englishman. The Iberians were particularly prized for their seamanship, while northern Europeans—Germans, Dutch, and English—were recruited for their skills in handling the ships' guns. Fonseca's influence with the king did enable him to force upon Magellan three Spanish captains: Gaspar de Quesada, Luis de Mendoza, and Juan de Cartagena, Fonseca's son. Cartagena's cousin Antonio de Coca was made the fleet's treasurer. Geronimo Guerra, Haro's illegitimate son, was its accountant. Estevão Gomes, who had hoped to command the expedition along with Cartagena, was made chief pilot; like Cartagena, he disliked and resented

A 1520 engraving of a sailing ship, of the general type that the Portuguese and Spanish called naos. Naos were bigger than caravels, with more space for cargo and crew, but they could be rigged with lateen or square sails. The ships Magellan took on his great voyage probably looked similar to this one.

Magellan. Both men listened with avid interest to Haro's suggestion that Magellan might be deposed as leader once the fleet was out to sea. Events were to demonstrate that the masters-at-arms of the *Trinidad* and the *San Antonio*, Gonzalo Gomez de Espinosa and Juan de Lloriaga, were just about the only trustworthy Spanish officers in the fleet. Of course, Magellan had complete confidence in João Serrão, in his cousin Alvaro de Mesquita, and in his brother-in-law Duarte Barbosa.

One of the most interesting members of the expedition—and, in retrospect, one of the most important—was Antonio Pigafetta, a gentleman from Venice who asked Magellan for a berth on the flagship. He demanded no pay and said only that he was curious to see the wonders of the world and "the very great and awful things of the

A bust of Antonio Pigafetta, the Venetian gentleman-adventurer who signed on with Magellan's crew. Fortunately, Pigafetta was 1 of the 18 men to complete the circumnavigation of the world, for his "book treating of all the things that had occurred on our voyage" is a complete and fascinating account of the expedition.

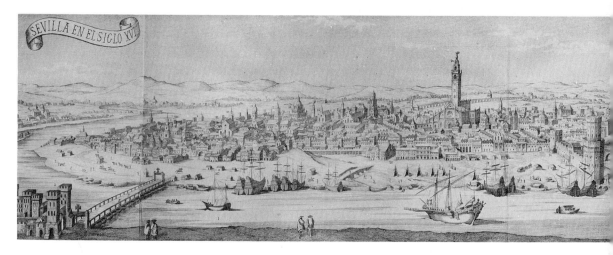

SEVILLA EN EL SIGLO XVI

A 16th-century depiction of the Spanish city of Seville, where Magellan prepared his fleet for its great voyage.

ocean." It is quite likely that he was in the pay of the Venetian trading companies, seeking not only adventure and wondrous sights but also information about what Spain was doing and what Magellan might find. Nevertheless, Magellan granted him permission to enlist. Whatever his motives, Pigafetta proved to be both tough and loyal. Best of all, he was a keen observer and kept a journal of the voyage, which he later turned into a book. Pigafetta's journal made Magellan's the best known of all the Renaissance voyages of discovery.

The task of repairing, provisioning, and manning the ships dragged on at the city of Seville for more than a year. (A Portuguese agent reported delightedly that Magellan's vessels were "very old and patched up" and that he "would not care to sail to the Canaries in such old crates; their ribs are as soft as butter.") Magellan's son, Rodrigo, was born during this time, and Beatriz became pregnant with a second child. That child was stillborn, but by then Magellan was no longer in Spain. King Charles, who assumed the additional title of Emperor Charles V of the Holy Roman Empire in 1519, had grown impatient for the departure of his explorers. At last he declared imperiously that the fleet would set sail on August 10, 1519.

Streto patagonico

Capo defeado

Mare oceano

Mare pis o

Capo da le ij. m. vir.

Porto di fanto Juliano

Regione patagonia

avo Di S.ta M.

To the Bottom
of the World

On the day appointed by the king, the captains and crews attended a farewell Mass at the Church of Santa Maria de la Victoria in the dockyards of Seville. Magellan swore loyalty to the king; the other captains swore to "follow the course of the captain-general and obey him in all things," although it is fairly certain that at least some of them had no intention of doing so; and the ships cast off at midday amid much pomp and circumstance. The voyage had not really begun, however—the fleet departed from Seville in obedience to the king's orders, but it went only as far as Sanlucar de Barrameda, 75 miles (120 kilometers) down the Guadalquivir River. There, where the river enters the sea, the fleet remained for more than five weeks while last-minute attempts were made to complete the provisioning of the ships.

During this time, Magellan drew up a will, carefully arranging that in the event of his death his estate—chiefly consisting of any islands or treasures he might acquire during the voyage—would be divided among his wife, his children, his sister Isabel and her children, and various churches. He bequeathed Henrique his freedom and a gift of money upon his master's death, and he also left a substantial sum to a young man named Cristóbal Rebelo, who served as Magellan's page on the voyage and is generally believed to have been his illegitimate son, although no one knows when or where Magellan fathered him or

Pigafetta's map of the Strait of Magellan, which he has labeled "Streto patagonico," or Patagonian Strait.

who his mother was. The will is a lengthy and detailed document, but unfortunately for the Barbosa and Magellan families its provisions were never carried out.

On September 20, the fleet was as ready as it would ever be. An offshore wind blew up, and a clerk in the Casa de Antillas noted in his ledger that "5 ships and 277 men embarked." This time, the voyage had begun in earnest.

The first landfall was the Canary Islands, a Spanish possession off the northwest coast of Africa, where water, wood, and vegetables were loaded aboard the ships. There Magellan received a disturbing message from the captain of a fast ship that had been sent out to overtake the fleet. The message was a warning from Diogo Barbosa, his father-in-law, who said that the Spanish captains were planning to kill the captain-general. Not long after the fleet left the Canaries, Magellan gave them an opportunity to do so.

He wanted to set a southward course, hugging the African coastline before striking out across the Atlantic, in the hope of avoiding any ships that King Manoel of Portugal might have sent out to intercept him. The Spanish captains, however, insisted on a more direct southwesterly course. Pretending meekness, Magellan agreed to the course they set. Three days out of the Canaries, he abruptly shifted his course to the south. Serrão followed in the *Santiago* leaving the Spanish captains no choice but to do likewise or be left behind altogether. Perhaps Magellan wanted to provoke an act of open rebellion by the Spaniards so that he could retaliate; if so, he soon succeeded. The Spaniards grew more discontented by the day. In November, soon after the fleet crossed the equator, all the captains met in Magellan's cabin aboard the *Trinidad* for the court-martial of one of the junior officers. After that business was concluded, Cartagena began complaining about the southward course. When he declared that he would no longer follow the captain-general, Magellan raised his

(continued on page 81)

Seeing the World

A 16th-century Italian portrait of Magellan.

If Magellan's voyage did not literally change the world, it did the closest thing to it—it changed the way human beings saw their planet. Magellan's circumnavigation was the culmination of the great age of Iberian exploration that was ushered in by the Portuguese prince Henry the Navigator in 1419 and fueled, over the next century, by equal parts economic self-interest, as represented by the desire of Europe's monarchs and merchants to reach the spice-rich Indies, and scientific curiosity. It is fitting that this epic journey was conducted by a Portuguese mariner sailing under the Spanish flag, for it was in their desire for their own route to the Orient that the Spanish monarchs Ferdinand and Isabella, following Portugal's lead, sponsored the voyages of Christopher Columbus, whose discoveries gave Spain the foundation of an overseas empire that quickly enabled it to rival its Iberian neighbor as Europe's foremost power. Magellan's circumnavigation yielded less immediate dividends, in the terms of which monarchs and merchants were accustomed to thinking of them, but it was no less important. It gave man his most comprehensive glimpse to that point of the world's dimensions and character—the breadth of its oceans, the sweep of its continents, and the awe-inspiring variety of life with which it was inhabited.

A circa-1600 map of Europe, Africa, and the Americas. Many of these regions were known to Europeans before Magellan's voyage, but the circum-navigator's journey gave Europe its first real idea of the vastness of the Pacific.

A 14th-century French painting of a caravan in the Levant, as the countries bordering eastern Mediterranean are sometimes known. Camel caravans were often used to carry spices from the Indies to market in Baghdad,

This 15th-century painting of the Spanish monarchs Ferdinand and Isabella by an anonymous Spanish artist casts the queen in the role of the Virgin Mary with the Christ child. In urging the monarchs to fund his voyage, Columbus appealed to Isabella's renowned piety by telling her that he would convert the peoples of the Indies.

A 16th-century engraving of
Magellan's fleet in the Pacific.
Most of the days he spent on
the world's greatest ocean were
far less tranquil.

This 16th-century Dutch map of the Strait of Magellan includes drawings of the exotic creatures found there. The strait proved to be of less import than Magellan had foretold, primarily because the Pacific's great size made the western route to the Indies impractical.

This map of lower South America and the Strait of Magellan was drawn soon after Magellan's voyage. It portrays the strait as a relatively open, easily negotiated passage.

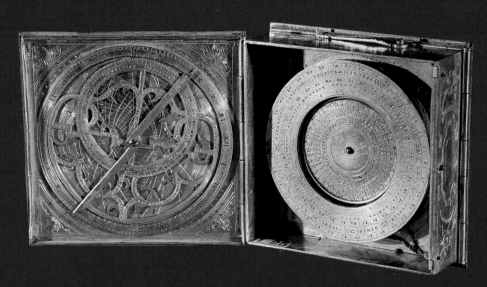

Spanish monarch Philip II inherited this ornate case and nautical calendar from his father, Charles I, who sponsored Magellan's voyage. Magellan's own navigational tools were probably less elaborate.

A 16th-century map of the world. Running vertically near the center of the chart is the line established by the Treaty of Tordesillas, which ostensibly divided the oceans between Portugal and Spain. It was this demarcation that forced Spain to seek a westward route to the Indies, a quest that led to Magellan's circumnavigation of the globe.

(continued from page 72)

hand. At that signal, the *Trinidad's* master-at-arms, Duarte Barbosa, and Cristóbal Rebelo ran into the cabin with drawn swords. Magellan seized Cartagena, accused him of disobeying a direct order, and had him thrown into the stocks (a wooden frame that imprisoned the legs) like a common seaman; Cartagena's supporters, Mendoza and Quesada, were helpless to intervene. Magellan then relieved Cartagena of the command of the *San Antonio*, replacing him with Antonio de Coca. In terms of loyalty, Coca was not much of an improvement, but for the time being Magellan's swift response to Cartagena's insubordination had firmly established his authority over the fleet.

Magellan had much more to contend with than shipboard politics, however. In October, before the fleet reached the equator, it was lashed by a series of squalls. Unable to make headway against the stormy seas, the vessels rolled and wallowed for weeks, or, as Pigafetta put it, "We went up and down in the sea until good weather came." During some of these storms, electrical discharges occurred at the tips of the ships' masts and yardarms. Called "St. Elmo's fire," these luminous globes of light

During storms at sea, St. Elmo's fire—electrical discharges that appeared at the tips of masts and spars—often consoled sailors, who believed that it announced the presence of their patron saint. St. Elmo was a 12th-century Dominican priest who preached and ministered to the sailors of northwest Spain.

were believed to be signs of good favor from St. Elmo, the patron saint of seamen. Describing one especially severe storm, Pigafetta reports that "the body of St. Elmo appeared in the form of a lighted torch at the height of the maintop, and remained there more than two hours and a half, to the comfort of us all. For we were in tears, expecting only the hour of death. And when this holy light was about to leave us, it was so bright to the eyes of all that we were for more than a quarter of an hour as blind men calling for mercy. For without any doubt no man thought that he would escape from that storm."

Once the tempests died down, the vessels emerged into the broad belt of calm, tropical ocean that is sometimes called the doldrums. Here, the sun blazed down from a cloudless sky, and the winds died. Pigafetta noted that large sharks followed the fleet. "They have terrible teeth," he wrote, "and eat men when they find them alive or dead

The dramatic entrance to the beautiful harbor at Rio de Janeiro, where Magellan's crew spent two enchanting weeks in December 1519 until the captain-general insisted that they push on in search of the strait.

in the sea." With meat rotting and men fainting in the holds from the heat, the ships lolled in the doldrums for 3 weeks, advancing only about 10 miles, slowly drifting on the sluggish south equatorial current. But then the sails swelled with the steady east-to-west trade winds, and the fleet made for Brazil. On December 6, a colorful land bird flew across the ships' path. On December 7, the men could smell the moist, earthy forests of South America, although the horizon remained empty. On December 8, a lookout sighted land.

Magellan made landfall in Brazil near the present-day city of Recife, in Portuguese territory. Anxious to avoid the attentions of the Portuguese, he ordered the fleet to proceed southward without delay. João Lopes Carvalho, a pilot who had accompanied João of Lisbon's expedition to those waters, was put in charge of setting the *Trinidad*'s course along the reef- and shoal-strewn coast; the other vessels followed in its wake. On December 13, the five ships rounded a cape and sailed into one of the most majestic and beautiful harbors in the world, a deep blue channel fringed with white beaches and dramatic forested peaks. Magellan named the bay Santa Luzia, because he entered it on the feast day of St. Lucy, but today it is called Rio de Janeiro, or "River of January," the name given it earlier by Coelho and Vespucci.

The fleet spent two delightful weeks in Rio—for some of the men, the last good time they enjoyed. The amiable Guaraní Indians were even more friendly than usual because the fleet happened to arrive the day after a rainfall that ended a 12-week drought and the Indians associated the arrival of the white men with the coming of the rain. Barter became commonplace once the men discovered that the Indians were happy to trade fruit, sugar cane, chickens, fish, and pigs—a welcome and healthy change from the shipboard diet—for metal or manufactured items. "For a bell or leather lace," Pigafetta wrote, "they gave as many fish as ten men could have eaten. . . . And for a king of playing cards, of the kind used in Italy, they gave me five fowls, and even thought they had cheated me." An even brisker exchange soon sprang up: A man could obtain the favors of any willing and unmarried Guaraní woman in exchange for a cheap pocketknife, paid to her brothers. The puritanical Magellan appears not to have taken part in the nightly debauches ashore, in which even the priests participated until they were dragged back to the ships by the masters-at-arms, and he sternly ordered the ships searched and all women ejected before the fleet set sail.

Pigafetta called the region the land of Verzin, which was its Indian name. It was here that he had his first opportunity to observe a people and a culture that were wholly new to him, and he devoted several pages of his narrative to describing them. He tells how the Guaraní lived in "fairly long houses" and slept "in nets of cotton, which they call in their language *Amache*" (*amache* eventually became the source of the English word "hammock"). He also wrote of their great skill in boat making, of how the men and women painted themselves "with fire all over the body and face" (by this he meant that they tattooed themselves), and of how they smoked and then ate enemies taken in battle: "They do not eat the whole body of the man taken, but eat it piece by piece. For fear that he be not tasted, they cut him up in pieces which they put to dry in the chimney, and every day they cut off a small piece and eat it with their ordinary food to call to mind their enemies." Pigafetta even made a list of eight words in the language of Verzin. Subsequent travelers found the vocabularies he compiled useful; modern anthropologists found them surprisingly accurate.

While the fleet was at Rio, Cartagena acted up again. Coca released Cartagena, who had been entrusted to Mendoza for safekeeping, and together the Spaniards tried to stir up a revolt against Magellan. Because they were Fonseca's relatives, the captain-general was reluctant to punish

Coca and Cartagena too severely, so once again he turned them over to Mendoza. This time, however, he appointed his cousin, Alvaro de Mesquita, captain of the *San Antonio*.

After leaving Rio, the fleet made good time along the coast. Whenever a bay or a river mouth was spotted, Magellan sent a ship or a longboat in to investigate, each time hoping that he had found el paso. Each time he was disappointed. In January 1520, Carvalho sighted a familiar landmark, Cape Santa María. Upon rounding this headland, Magellan saw a vast reach of open water running away to the west—right where Juan de Solís and João of Lisbon said the strait was to be found. He sent the *Santiago*

A *late-16th-century engraving of an encounter between Dutch explorers and outsized, bearded Indians in the Strait of Magellan. Although the Dutch who explored Patagonia after Magellan echoed Pigafetta's reports of unusually tall native inhabitants, no archaeological evidence confirming these reports has ever been discovered.*

One hundred years after Magellan discovered el paso, a Dutch artist portrayed the curiosities to be found there, including seals, penguins, ostriches, guanacos, and the skeletons of giant Indians.

to probe this new waterway. A few days later, the *Santiago* came back and reported that the channel had grown narrow and shallow, and that the water inland was fresh, meaning that it was a river, not a sea passage. Magellan sent a ship's boat still farther upstream, hoping it would find some connection to the sea, but at last he was forced to admit that this great waterway was not the strait. It was, in fact, the wide mouth of the river that is today called the Río de la Plata. According to Pigafetta, the Río de la Plata region was inhabited by tall cannibal Indians, the very ones who "ate a Spanish captain named Juan de Solís." Seven small islands were found in the river mouth, and on one of them, he reported, "precious stones are found"—although he did not say whether he had found any. But the river was not the strait, and sometime early in February Magellan ordered the fleet south again along the coast.

They passed some small islands, where lived creatures unlike any they had ever seen. Pigafetta called them black geese and sea wolves, and said of the "wolves" that "if these animals could run, they would be very fierce and cruel. But they do not leave the water, where they swim and live on fish." The black geese were penguins, and the sea wolves were sea lions. For the first time, Europeans were nearing the borders of the Antarctic realm, and everything they saw along the bleak and desolate coast was alien and new. Under orders from the captain-general, the ships stayed close to the rocky shore, where they were battered by high tides and treacherous winds; he wanted no bay or indentation in the coast to pass untested. But each time a bay or a westward curve in the coastline raised hopes

When Magellan sent João Serrão south from Port San Julián to reconnoiter the coast, a fierce storm wrecked the Santiago *in the mouth of the Santa Cruz River.*

that the strait had been found at last, those hopes proved to be in vain.

Sailing conditions worsened day by day. The southern winter was drawing on. Sleet and snow lashed the always-rough waters off the coast of southern Argentina; icebergs loomed up in the fog. Storms scattered the fleet on at least three occasions, the *Santiago*'s mast was torn out, and the *San Antonio* sprang a large leak. Chroniclers agree that Magellan's officers, and even some of the common sailors, tried several times to persuade him to turn back, either to seek the Spice Islands by the milder eastern route or to retreat to warm winter quarters in Rio, but he simply refused. Out of confidence that his belief in the strait would eventually be justified, or simple stubbornness, or perhaps a degree of obsession that bordered on madness, he forced the fleet on—until at the end of March the five ships made anchor at Port San Julián, and the revolt of the Spanish captains was thwarted with the executioner's sword. The winter months of April through September were passed at Port San Julián and at Santa Cruz, the site Serrão discovered when the *Santiago* was lost.

At Port San Julián, Pigafetta once again demonstrated his lively curiosity about the inhabitants of what was to him a very strange land. When, after several months, an Indian man approached the fleet, the chronicler took careful note of his appearance: "He had a very large face, painted round with red, and his eyes also were painted round with yellow, and in the middle of his cheeks he had two hearts painted. He had hardly any hairs on his head, and they were painted white." The Indian's clothes (made of guanaco skins) and weapons (short bows and arrows made of cane) received scrutiny also. Eventually, Pigafetta was able to compile a list of 90 words in the local Indian language.

But here, as elsewhere in his journey around the world, the Italian chronicler seems to have been most interested in the behavior and beliefs of the peoples he encountered. Pigafetta recorded in detail the slow process of winning the Indians' confidence with gifts and soothing gestures—and how the Europeans betrayed that trust by taking several Indians prisoner. He said that the Indians included thistles in their diets, and that they treated stomachaches by thrusting arrows down their throats to make themselves vomit. He also seems to have learned something of their religious thinking, for he wrote: "When one of them dies, ten or twelve devils appear, and dance around the dead man. And it seems they are painted. And one of these devils is much taller than the others, and makes much more noise, and rejoices much more than the others. And from this the giants [that is, the natives] took the fashion of painting themselves on the face and body, as has been said." According to Pigafetta, the ordinary devils were called *Cheleule* and the large one was called *Setebos*. This revelation made its way into literary history when William Shakespeare gave the name "Setebos" to the god worshiped by the witch Sycorax and her son Caliban in *The Tempest* (1611); two and a half centuries later, Robert Browning based his philosophical poem "Caliban upon Setebos" (1860) on Shakespeare's play, which in turn was indirectly based on Pigafetta's narrative.

On October 18, 1520, the fleet set sail from Santa Cruz. Despite Magellan's firmness at Port San Julián, opposition continued. Estevão Gomes, the pilot who had been Cristóbal de Haro's original choice for expedition leader, protested against the continuation of the southward course. It was obvious that Magellan did not know for sure that the strait existed, he said, or where it was, and it would be better to put the captain-general in irons, return to Port San Julián to look for Cartagena, and then make for the Spice Islands by the Portuguese route. Gomes was not able to muster any support, however, and Magellan ignored his complaints. The fleet stood out to the south.

(continued on page 92)

Las Casas reported that because Magellan's "person did not carry much authority . . . people thought they could put it over him for want of prudence and courage," but the mariners who witnessed firsthand his steely determination in the strait and the Pacific knew better.

The Mystery of the Patagonian Giants

One of the biggest geographic sensations of the 16th century—and one of the biggest geographic puzzles ever since—is Pigafetta's account of the giant men of Patagonia. The Italian wrote that the Indians of Port San Julián were so tall that "the tallest of us only came up to his waist." One Indian, who became especially friendly with the crewmen, was nicknamed Juan the Giant. Antonio de Herrera y Tordesillas, the official Spanish historian of the voyage, wrote an account based on interviews with the survivors in which he asserted that a number of the Indians visited Magellan's ships and that the smallest of them was taller than the tallest of the Europeans. Magellan named these Indians Patagonians, from *patagon*, the Portuguese word for "large foot" or "clumsy foot." The name, which referred either to the natives' large feet or to the wrappings of guanaco hide that they wore as crude boots, survives today as Patagonia, a general term for the plains region of southern Argentina and Chile.

Pigafetta devoted many pages of his narrative to a description of the giants' appearance and customs; unfortunately, accurate though the Italian was in many other respects, not a bit of physical evidence has ever been found to support his statements about the size of the Indians. Many voyagers who came after Pigafetta, however, echoed his account. By the early years of the 17th century, the Englishmen Sir Francis Drake and Anthony Knyvet, the Spaniard Pedro Sarmiento de Gamboa, and the Dutchmen Sebald de Weert and Joris van Spilbergen had all claimed to have seen giants—or at least extremely tall men—near the strait. In 1615, the Dutch navigators Jan Schouten and Jakob Le Maire dug up an Indian grave on the coast of Patagonia and claimed that it held the bones of men 10 or 11 feet (3.5 meters) tall. As late as 1765, seamen who sailed the strait under the English commodore John Byron claimed to have seen giants eight or even nine feet (two and a half or three meters) in height. So popular were accounts of the Patagonian giants in Europe that some scholars believe they were one of the sources of Jonathan Swift's Brobdingnagian giants in the satire *Gulliver's Travels* (1726).

In the meantime, contrary accounts were also piling up. Sir John Narborough of England spent 10 months in Patagonia in 1670 and reported that the people there were "not taller than Englishmen generally are." In 1741, two English naval officers wrote that the Indians of the strait "are people of a middle stature." The English naturalist Charles Darwin, generally agreed to be an accurate observer, visited Patagonia in 1834 and said of the local Tehuelche Indian men: "On an average their height is about six feet, with some men taller and only a few shorter."

Were there really giants in Patagonia when Magellan arrived there? Most likely, no, but the Tehuelche, like many Native American people, are of a height that is on average somewhat greater than that of Mediterranean peoples and they are definitely taller than the Guaraní Indians, whom Pigafetta had seen in Rio. It is likely, too, that the ablest warriors, who might have been the tallest men, were sent out to reconnoiter the strange ships and Europeans. In addition, Darwin speculated that the Indians looked taller than they really were because they wore their hair long and were clothed in long, flowing robes. Most modern scholars believe that Pigafetta probably exaggerated to impress his audience and that later voyagers and chroniclers followed his lead. Yet some of the peoples of southern South America really are, and were, of greater stature than many Europeans—so the stories of Patagonian giants were not entirely tall tales.

Dutch mariners who sailed through the Strait of Magellan in the early 17th century reportedly exhumed the remains of a giant Indian (center).

The Strait of Magellan's imposing landscape worked its magic on Pigafetta, who concluded, "I believe that there is not a more beautiful or better strait in the world than that one."

(continued from page 89)

Three days later, on St. Ursula's feast day, the fleet rounded a large cape, which Magellan named the Cape of the Eleven Thousand Virgins because St. Ursula was believed to have been the leader of 11,000 virgin martyrs who were killed by Huns in the 4th or 5th century. Beyond the cape was a large curve of water, surrounded by high cliffs and mountains. To all but Magellan, it was clear that this was just another bay, with no way out except the way the ships had come in. Unconvinced, the captain-general ordered the *Concepción* and the *San Antonio* to explore the bay's farther reaches. To the dismay of all, no sooner had the two vessels set off into the bay than a gale rose, blowing them swiftly toward the wall of rock at its far end. The two ships' destruction seemed certain, but the crews of the *Trinidad* and the *Victoria* were themselves occupied in battling the storm and were unable to lend a hand. They battled the storm for 48 hours; then, giving the *Concepción* and the *San Antonio* up for lost, they prepared to leave the bay. At that moment, Pigafetta wrote, "We saw the two ships approaching under full sail and flying their banners, coming toward us. When near us, they suddenly discharged their ordnance, at which we very joyously greeted them in the same way. And then we all, thanking God and the Virgin Mary, went forward."

Blown by the storm toward the rock wall of the bay, the *Concepción* and the *San Antonio* would have been destroyed had not their pilots spied a small waterway, which they thought was a creek. They steered for it in desperation, only to find that it was a narrow channel, screened from view of the open sea by a cliff, that opened into a second wide bay like a lake. The western end of that bay was a second narrow channel. This led in turn to yet another broad, lakelike reach. The captains tested the water and found that it still contained salt. As soon as the winds died down and the captains could retrace their path, they made for the captain-general and the rest of the fleet with the joyous news that the strait had been discovered at last. Because el paso had been found on All Saints' Day, November 1, Magellan devoutly named it the Strait of All Saints, but the mapmakers and chroniclers who recorded his achievement have always called it the Strait of Magellan, the name by which it is known today.

An imaginative rendition of the discovery of the strait. Pigafetta reported that upon learning that el paso opened into the South Sea, Magellan "wept with joy."

Across the Endless Sea

Although Magellan had found the strait, he was yet to get safely through it. The Strait of Magellan is not a simple gap between 2 land masses, like the Strait of Gibraltar, or a straight and open passage between 2 coasts, like the Strait of Malacca, but a twisting 334-mile (534-kilometer) channel between the southern tip of the South American mainland and a cluster of large and small islands that are the tops of submerged mountains. The channel trends southwest, then turns sharply northwest, wide in places and then suddenly narrow again. Numerous islands, fjords, and bays along the way make it difficult for even the experienced mariners of today, with navigational charts and buoys to guide them, to pick out the right channel. In addition, the strait is scoured by high tides, strong currents, and abrupt winds, making it extremely hazardous for vessels under sail power alone; the current guide to navigation for the strait advises only motor vessels to try it.

Captains Mesquita and Serrão had seen enough of this maze of water and rock to be sure that it would be difficult sailing. Furthermore, the fleet carried food for only two months—and who knew how much longer it would take to reach the Moluccas? Gomes advocated marking the location of the strait on the fleet's charts, making for the Moluccas by the certain eastward route, and returning to attempt the strait another day. Not surprisingly, Magellan was not about to be deterred. According to most accounts,

The captain-general with the tools of his trade, a quadrant and a nautical chart.

he declared that they would continue through the strait and beyond even if they were reduced to eating the leather wrappings from the masts.

It took the fleet all of November to pick its way through the strait. They saw no people, although apparently they did find the remains of a village, or perhaps a graveyard, at one landing place in the eastern part of the strait, and at night they sighted fires away to the left, on the strait's south side. They gave the land the name Tierra de los Fuegos, or Land of the Fires. Today it is still called Tierra del Fuego; it is a large island divided between Argentina and Chile. All the while the scenery grew grander, as the hills and grassy plains of eastern Patagonia gave way to 1,000-foot (300-meter) cliffs, glaciers spilling into the sea, snow-covered peaks, and perpetually damp forests of dwarf birch and moss. Good anchorages were plentiful, as were fresh water, sardines, firewood, and edible herbs. Said Pigafetta, "I think there is in the world no more beautiful country or better place than that."

Not all the members of the expedition agreed with Pigafetta's assessment, and midway through the strait Magellan lost another ship. He sent the *Concepción* and the *San Antonio* to scout one fork in the channel while the *Trinidad* and the *Victoria* explored another. After a few days of this, Magellan sent a few men in one of the *Trinidad*'s boats to probe the channel ahead, hoping that they would sight the far end of the strait. "They spent three days going and returning," says Pigafetta, "and told us that they had found the cape and the great and wide sea. Wherefore the captain, for the joy that he had, began to weep and gave this cape the name Cabo Deseado [Cape of Desire], as a thing much desired and long sought." But the *San Antonio* failed to appear at the agreed-upon meeting place, and Captain Serrão of the *Concepción* reported that he had lost sight of the other ship after dark one night. Magellan searched the inlets and channels for the *San Antonio* for nearly three weeks, even sending one of the ships all the way back to the Cape of the Eleven Thousand Virgins to look for it. No trace was found. Finally, the captain-general asked the fleet's astrologer, Andres de San Martín, to solve the mystery. San Martín gave an answer based as much on common sense as on the positions of the planets—he said that Gomes, the pilot of the *San Antonio*, had overpowered Captain Mesquita and taken the ship back to Spain. The astrologer was right; the troublemakers Gomes and Guerra had placed the unlucky Captain Mesquita in irons and turned for home. They arrived in Spain in May 1521.

The loss of the *San Antonio* was a severe blow, for that ship held a large portion of the fleet's provisions. The ocean was waiting at the end of the strait, however, and Magellan ordered the men to stock the ships with abundant stores of fish, birds, and game. He ignored the wild celery and other edible plants that grow plentifully along the strait; this, although he did not know it, contributed to the agonies his men were soon to suffer.

A Dutch map from the early 17th century shows a fleet emerging from the Strait of Magellan into the South Sea. Once found, el paso proved to be of less practical use than Magellan and others had predicted.

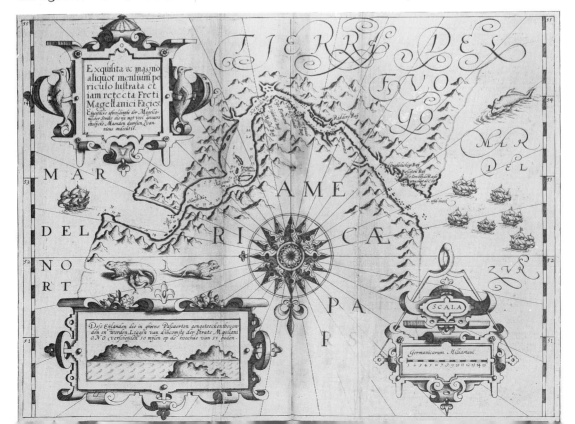

On November 28, 1520, the *Trinidad*, the *Concepción*, and the *Victoria* sailed through heavy breakers at the mouth of the strait into the open sea beyond Cabo Deseado. Here at last was Balboa's "South Sea"; Magellan and his men were the first Europeans to enter it. Magellan named it the Mar Pacifico, or peaceful sea. The name was well chosen, for in the entire crossing of the Pacific the fleet encountered no storms. Its problems were of a different nature entirely.

Magellan was quite right in expecting to find the Moluccas and the rest of Asia on the far side of the Pacific. But neither he nor any other European had the slightest inkling of the vastness of the Pacific world that now opened up before them. All their estimates of the ocean's size fell short of the truth by at least 80 percent. The Pacific Ocean is greater in area than all the earth's land masses combined and more than twice the size of the Atlantic; it stretches more than a third of the way around the planet. Although

A peaceable kingdom of the creatures of the sea greets Magellan's fleet upon its entrance into the Pacific in this 16th-century artwork. The newly discovered ocean's tranquility led Magellan to name it the Pacific, but his passage proved to be anything but calm.

it is dotted with thousands of islands, many of them inhabited by the seafaring peoples of Polynesia, these lands and their cultures were completely unknown to the Europeans of Magellan's time. When their three ships set forth into this great mystery, Magellan's men confidently expected to reach the spices and pleasures of the Moluccas in a few weeks at most.

They headed north at first, to escape the sub-Antarctic cold. They remained within sight of the coast of present-day Chile to a point just north of the modern city of Valdivia, and then, in the middle of December, struck out into the open sea. Magellan's course was ideal in one respect, for it kept favorable winds at his back and kept him clear of dangerous coral atolls that might have ripped the bottoms out of his ships, but in another respect it was supremely unfortunate, for it carried the fleet just out of sight of many of the most fruitful and hospitable of the Pacific islands. Magellan missed the Juan Fernández islands, Easter Island, and other places where his men could have obtained fresh water and food, and it was not long before they felt the lack of these foodstuffs. It was 98 days from leaving the strait before the small fleet made land again for any significant period of time. During that time the hastily cured flesh of the penguins and guanacos that had been caught in the strait rotted in the stinking holds. Biscuit crumbled into powder that was soon crawling with worms and stained with the urine of rats, and the water in the barrels turned yellow and foul. Hunger and thirst tormented the men, who gnawed greedily at even these vile rations. The holds were searched for rats; a fresh one sold for half a gold ducat or more—and, says Pigafetta, "some of us could not get enough." Fulfilling his vow, Magellan pressed onward even after he and his men were reduced to eating the leather wrappings from the masts, which they did after soaking them in the sea for three or four days to soften them and then roasting them on hot

(continued on page 102)

Latitude, Longitude, and Luck

Over centuries of mapmaking, cartographers have devised a system for pinpointing the location of any spot on the earth's surface. That system is the grid work of horizontal and vertical lines that can be seen to overlay the outlines of the continents and seas on almost all maps. The horizontal lines run east-west and are called lines of latitude. The latitude of a place is simply its distance north or south of the equator—that is, which line of latitude crosses it. The vertical lines (which curve to meet at the poles on globes and certain kinds of maps) run north-south and are called lines of longitude, or meridians. A place's longitude is its distance east or west of one particular meridian that runs through Greenwich, England. Together, latitude and longitude determine a place's location on a map in a way that enables anyone to find it.

The navigators of Magellan's day did reasonably well with latitude. Using an instrument called an astrolabe, which was invented by the ancient Greeks, or a simplified version of it called the cross-staff, they measured the angle between the horizon and the sun or a fixed star. From this measurement, they were able to calculate their latitude to within 1 degree (a degree is $1/360$th of the distance around the world, about 69 miles or 111 kilometers). Thus Magellan and his contemporaries usually knew just about how far south or north of the equator they were. But once out of sight of known landmarks, they had a lot of trouble determining how far east or west of a desired location they might be, because longitude is more difficult than latitude to measure.

Accurate calculation of longitude requires accurate timepieces, which did not exist in the 1520s. Not until the Englishman John Harrison invented the marine chronometer in the mid-18th century was precise longitudinal measurement possible at sea. Until then, mariners made do with rough estimates of longitude, using three tools: the compass, which identified the direction of the course; the hourglass, which was used to measure the passage of time; and the log line, a chunk of wood tied at a set position on a rope.

A seaman threw the log line overboard; then, by seeing how long it took for the wood to disappear, he could make a guess at his ship's speed. (The record of log line measurements was called the "log," a term that came to be used for all the captain's navigational records.)

Together with the daily measurement of latitude, the three factors of speed, time, and direction were used to plot the ship's position on the sea chart. If one factor were off—if the seaman estimated the speed wrongly, say, or if a sailor on night watch held the hourglass under his shirt to warm it, causing the glass to expand and the sand to flow through it faster, which in turn meant that his spell of watch duty would end early—then the entire calculation was wrong. Because each day's calculation was based on that of the preceding day, the magnitude of a single error often grew larger over the course of a voyage.

This type of navigation, in which latitude can be judged fairly accurately but longitude is a series of more or less lucky guesses, is called *dead reckoning*. The term is apt, for mistakes in reckoning have caused the loss of hundreds of ships and the death of countless marines. When Magellan landed in the Philippines, he was on a southward course that would have taken him back into the latitude of the Moluccas, but because he was unable to measure his longitude accurately (and did not know the correct east-west position of the Moluccas in the first place), he had already overshot them by several degrees of longitude.

An ornate 17th-century astrolabe. By using an astrolabe to measure the angle between the horizon and a celestial body such as the sun or a star, mariners could calculate how far north or south of the equator they had sailed.

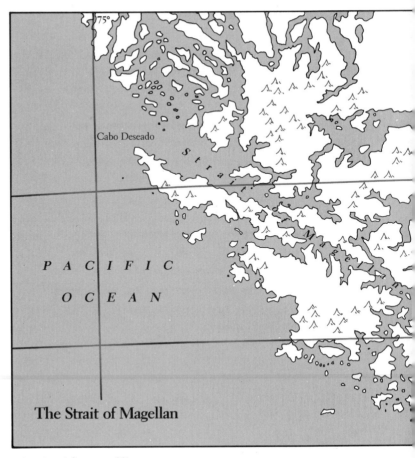

75°

Cabo Deseado

PACIFIC

OCEAN

The Strait of Magellan

(continued from page 99)

coals. Sawdust and wood chips supplemented the starve-lings' diet.

Soon, like many mariners in the early days of long voyages, they began to suffer from scurvy, a disease brought about by the lack of vitamin C in the diet. At sea, sailors ate mostly biscuit and preserved meat, with the occasional fish thrown in; aside from very limited amounts of jellies or dried fruits, which generally were reserved for the officers, their diet was devoid of vitamin C. Had Magellan loaded his ships with the wild celery and other plants he found in the strait, instead of with salted fish and meat, the suffering might have been less. But it was not until 250 years later that captains learned to carry lemons and limes, or other fruits and vegetables, to prevent scurvy. The disease ravaged Magellan's crew, causing the men's

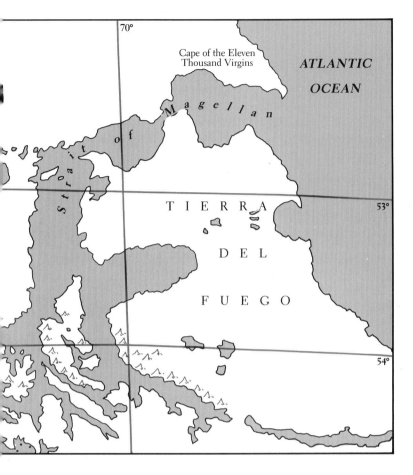

limbs and joints to ache and their gums to swell so much that they could not have eaten even if they had food. By mid-January 1521, one-third of the crew was too weak to walk. Then, they began to die. Pigafetta wrote that the first to go was a young Patagonian giant whom Magellan had managed to lure on board the *Trinidad* at Port San Julián. At least a dozen others died, perhaps as many as 20, and many more were too ill to work.

On January 24, 1521, the fleet sighted its first land since leaving South America. It was a barren, uninhabited island, probably Pukapuka at the northern end of the Tuamotu Archipelago. Had they sailed a bit to the south, they would have sighted the Tuamotus or Tahiti; a bit to the north, they would have seen the lush Marquesas Islands. But Magellan seems to have lacked the "divine guidance"

Pigafetta's rendering of Las Islas de Ladrones, *or the Isles of Thieves, as the weary voyagers dubbed Guam and Rota. Although appalled at the islanders' rapacity, the adventurers were impressed by their lateen-sailed outriggers.*

that Columbus credited with making his voyages such marvels of navigational prowess, and on Pukapuka (which they named St. Paul's) they found only crabs, fish, and the eggs of sea birds. There was no fresh water, but a timely rainfall let them refill their barrels. They sailed on.

On February 4, they sighted land again, most likely Vostok Island. Coconut palms beckoned from its shores, but the ships were unable to land; there was no shallow anchorage, and the currents swept them past. They called it the Isle of Sharks, for the huge sharks that they saw around it. Magellan called Vostok and Pukapuka together the Desaventuras, or "the unfortunate isles."

During the following week, the fleet crossed the equator for the second time, this time going north. Magellan knew that to linger along the equatorial line was to risk the doldrums again, so he continued north and west in a long arc that took his ships out of sight of the Marshall Islands and the Caroline Islands. Still the men sickened and died, and still the longed-for Moluccas failed to appear on the horizon. The rats were long gone; those who were strong enough to eat subsisted on sawdust. Then, on March 5, three islands were sighted. They were Guam, Saipan, and Rota, the southernmost islands of the Marianas chain.

The fleet anchored off Guam, but it immediately encountered difficulties. The inhabitants of the island canoed to the ships and swarmed over their sides. They were there not to fight but to scavenge, for they quickly made off with every bit of rope, metal, or wood they could pick up. Magellan lost his temper when they stole the ship's boat, and he ordered his crossbowmen to open fire. The islanders had never seen such weapons; when struck, they drew the large-headed crossbow bolts out, which killed them instantly. The survivors fled into the woods, and Magellan took 40 men ashore to confiscate all their food, burn their village, and reclaim the boat. Then, greatly strengthened by the fish, coconuts, bananas, and sweet potatoes they had taken from the islanders' huts, the trav-

elers raised anchor. Some of the natives followed them in
canoes, hurling insults and stones, but the ships made
away on a strong wind. The voyagers named Guam the
Isle of Thieves.

Magellan now set a southwestward course. The open,
seemingly endless sea stretched ahead. In all the Pacific
Ocean, Magellan had found only 5 islands, but now, 10
days after leaving the Isle of Thieves, the fleet came upon
2 green land masses in the blue sea. Beyond them lay
several others, and still more dotted the horizon. The fleet
had come upon a huge archipelago. Magellan named it
in honor of St. Lazarus, but in 1542 a Spanish explorer
renamed this 1,000-mile (1,600-kilometer) chain of 7,000
islands after the 15-year-old heir to the throne who would
become King Philip II of Spain. When he made landfall
at the edge of the Philippines, 108 days and 13,000 miles
(20,800 kilometers) from Cabo Deseado, Magellan had
truly crossed the Pacific at last. "And I believe that nev-
ermore will any man undertake to make such a voyage,"
wrote Pigafetta.

Magellan's voyage helped give the cartographers of all nations a clearer picture of the world's geography. This pre-1540 woodcut appeared in Sebastian Münster's Cosmographia, *the first detailed description of the world to appear in German.*

Magellan's Tragic Triumph

The fleet anchored at the small island of Homonhon, and tents were set up on shore for the sick. Friendly Filipino islanders approached and offered the men coconuts, fish, and palm wine, for which they were given red caps and mirrors. Several days later, they brought more food. On this occasion, they were accompanied by a chief who wore golden ornaments. The sight of gold was thrilling to the men, who had suffered so much in the hope of rich rewards, but Magellan cleverly warned them not to show too much interest in it, or they would drive up the price. (This strategy worked; by pretending not to value the precious metal, the Europeans eventually got the Filipinos to trade it for iron at a pound for a pound.)

Magellan's officers, including his friend Serrão, begged him to set off at once for the Moluccas, which could not now be very distant, and where Francisco Serrão was waiting with a warehouse full of spices. The men wanted to take their treasure and go home. But Magellan dismissed their pleas, announcing that they would explore the archipelago he had discovered and claimed for Spain. They made for the northwest, away from the Spice Islands. On March 28, they reached the island of Limasawa, where the people spoke a language that Henrique, Magellan's Malay slave, could understand. Here was proof positive, if any was needed, that they had rounded the world and had finally reached the eastern fringes of the known lands.

Magellan presented the wife of Rajah Humabon with this 13-inch wooden statue of the Christ Child upon her conversion to Christianity.

The ruler of Limasawa was a king, or rajah, named Colambu, who welcomed the newcomers to his country. He hosted a lavish feast on the beach for several of the ships' officers, at which rice, fish, pork, and palm wine were served in golden dishes. Pigafetta reports that he and one other European dined that night in the rajah's palace, and, he adds, "My companion made so good cheer in eating and drinking that he became intoxicated." Pigafetta spent the night with his companion at the palace, sleeping on a bed of reeds with a pillow of leaves. He described the clothing of the local inhabitants (which was scanty), their jewelry (which consisted of earrings of gold and ivory), their habits (like many Asians today, they chewed betel nut, a very mild intoxicant that turns the teeth and gums of users bright red), and their sexual practices (he said rather smugly that the Filipino women preferred the attentions of the Europeans to those of their own men). He had a high opinion of Colambu, calling him "the most handsome person whom we saw among those peoples." Pigafetta described the rajah this way: "He had very black hair to his shoulders, with a silk cloth on his head, and two large gold rings hanging from his ears. He wore a cotton cloth, embroidered with silk, which covered him from his waist to his knees. At his side he had a dagger, with a long handle, and all of gold, the sheath of which was of carved wood." Colambu also wore perfume and was either painted or tattooed all over. He and the captain-general got along well and even became blood brothers, each tasting the other's blood.

Colambu gave his permission for the fleet's priests to hold an Easter Sunday Mass at Limasawa. He and another local king attended and were impressed by the solemn ceremony—and by the roar of the ships' guns that Magellan ordered as a salute when the host was consecrated. The rajah made no objection when Magellan announced that he planned to erect a cross on a nearby hill. The Europeans and the Limasawans then made various agreements of trade and friendship, and Colambu offered to guide Magellan to Cebu, the capital of the islands. In return, Magellan sent some of his men to help Colambu's people harvest their rice. These initially harmonious relations gave no hint of the tragedy that was soon to unfold.

Upon arriving at Cebu, the men embarked on an orgy of barter and fornication. Magellan was introduced to Rajah Humabon, the overlord of the islands, but he refused to pay the tribute of gifts and fees that was customary for traders in the rajah's territory. This insult to his authority left the rajah inclined to deal harshly with Magellan, but a Siamese trader who was visiting Cebu advised him to be cautious in his treatment of the Europeans, because, he said, "These men are of those who have conquered Calicut, Malacca, and all India the Greater. If you give them good reception and treat them well, it will be well for you, but if you treat them ill, so much the worse it will be for you, as they have done at Calicut and at Malacca." Magellan reinforced this point by inviting Colambu and Hu-

The islanders of Homonhon and Limasawa, in the Philippines, rowed out to meet and trade with Magellan's fleet in long, narrow canoes like these. Magellan received a colder welcome at other islands.

mabon to the *Trinidad*, where he impressed them with a demonstration of Spanish armor and weapons.

On April 14, the fleet chaplains held a large Mass ashore. When some of the people showed interest in the service, wrote Pigafetta, "The captain told them that they should not become Christians for fear of us, or in order to please us, but that if they wished to become Christians, it should be with a good heart and for the love of God." Inspired either by the love of God or a desire to please his powerful visitor, or because he was impressed with the novel rites and ornaments of Christianity, Rajah Humabon asked to be baptized a Christian. So did Rajah Colambu. Then the local chiefs lined up to be converted, probably because Humabon had threatened them with death if they did not. More than 500 men followed suit. Finally, the rajah's chief wife and 50 of her ladies asked to be baptized. Magellan gave her a small wooden statue of the Christ Child. This statue, one of the most treasured relics of the Philippines, is preserved today in the Convent of Santo Niño in the city of Cebu; it is the only surviving object known to have belonged to Magellan. At about this time, Magellan took a religious dare: The brother of the crown prince was so ill that he could not walk, and Magellan offered to cure him if he would agree to burn all of his pagan idols after he was made well. The captain-general had the *Trinidad*'s priest baptize the sick man and sprinkle him with holy water, and then he gave him almond milk to drink. By great good fortune, the patient recovered. Five days later, he was able to walk, and he and his followers burned their idols, which Pigafetta described as hollow statues of painted wood with fanged faces like boars.

For days thereafter, the priests were kept busy baptizing new converts, until all the people of Cebu, and some of those from the nearby islands, had become Christians. Humabon ordered all his subjects to convert, and most obeyed, but Pigafetta reports that the Europeans felt com-

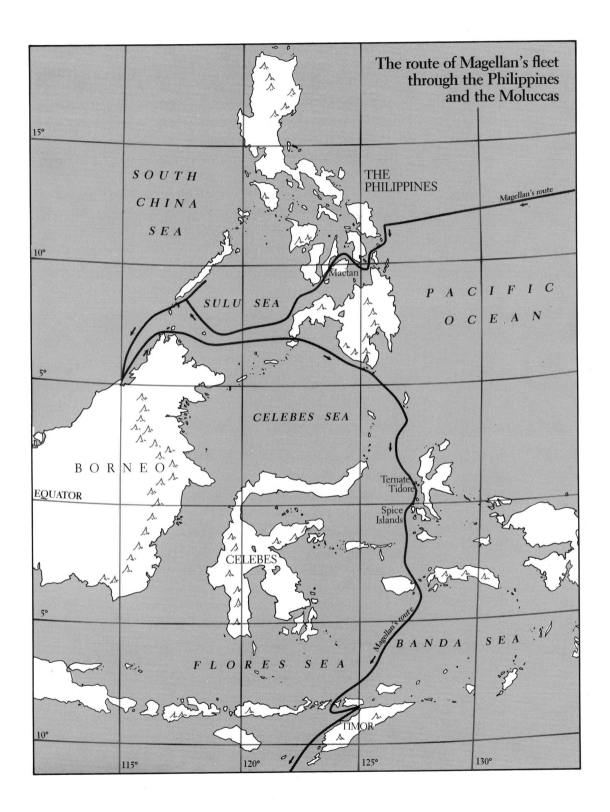

The route of Magellan's fleet
through the Philippines
and the Moluccas

SOUTH

CHINA

SEA

THE
PHILIPPINES

Magellan's route

PACIFIC

OCEAN

SULU SEA

Mactan

CELEBES SEA

BORNEO

EQUATOR

Ternate
Tidore

Spice
Islands

CELEBES

FLORES SEA

Magellan's route

BANDA SEA

TIMOR

15°

10°

5°

5°

10°

115°   120°   125°   130°

The death of Magellan, who was slain while defending the retreat of his men following his own ill-conceived attack on the island of Mactan. Although badly outnumbered, "as a good captain and a knight, [Magellan] still stood fast with some others, fighting thus for more than an hour," according to Pigafetta.

pelled to burn a village that refused baptism. "There we set up the cross, because those people were heathen," he continues. "And if they had been Moors [that is, Muslims] we should have put up a column, as a sign of greater achievement, for these Moors are more difficult to convert than the heathen."

Many words have been written about Magellan's furious burst of religious enthusiasm on Cebu, but it is unlikely that anyone will ever know what motivated him. Did this genuinely devout man believe that he had discovered a new purpose, a sense of spiritual mission? Did he feel that converting "the heathen" to Christ would make them better allies and trade partners? Or was he, perhaps, a bit emotionally unstable after his years of striving against human and natural obstacles to reach the East, and therefore too much inclined to enjoy the power and importance that these mass conversions gave him? Perhaps all the suggestions that historians have made contain some degree of truth. They remain speculation, however, while the facts that are known about the short remainder of Magellan's life tell a story of foolhardiness, bravery, and betrayal.

Lapulapu, a chieftain of the nearby island of Mactan, refused to recognize Humabon's overlordship—and, of course, he refused to adopt the strange new faith of Humabon's Western friends. A rival chieftain, perhaps hoping to gain control of Mactan, asked Magellan to punish Lapulapu, and Magellan agreed. Although Serrão and others urged him not to get involved in local politics, the captain-general, as was true in most matters, was not to be swayed. He took his ships to Mactan, where he asked for volunteers to attack Lapulapu's forts. About 50 or 60 men, including Pigafetta, Rebelo, and Espinosa, responded. At dawn on April 27, they rowed for the beach in three longboats. The ships waited at anchor a safe distance beyond spear shot, the officers and men lined up at their rails to watch. Rajah Colambu, Magellan's blood brother, brought some of his canoes and men, but Magellan ordered him not to interfere.

The assault on Mactan was a disaster. Whatever his other qualities, Magellan was a poor military strategist. The longboats got stuck on coral reefs at least 200 yards (183 meters) from the beach, and the invaders—many of them wearing heavy armor—had to wade ashore waist-deep in water. No sooner had they reached land than they were attacked by Lapulapu's men; Pigafetta says there were 3,500 of them. The actual number was probably something less, but the invaders were outnumbered many times over. The natives retreated as the Europeans advanced, but neither side could manage to inflict any casualties. Then Magellan sent two men to set fire to a nearby village. This so enraged Lapulapu's forces that they overwhelmed the two and killed them. The battle turned. Seeing that the Europeans were not invincible, the Filipinos pressed forward, launching a barrage of fire-hardened spears. They soon figured out to aim for their enemies' legs, which were not covered by armor, and Magellan's men began to fall. Some of them turned and made for the boats. The invasion became a retreat, then a rout.

According to Pigafetta, the battle-hardened captain-general held his ground, trying to muster enough fighters to cover the retreat of his men, for more than an hour. The Italian and Henrique were among the six or eight who remained at Magellan's side. Meanwhile, beyond the reef, Colambu paddled from ship to ship, begging the officers to go to Magellan's aid. It is probable that Carvalho and some of the other officers were by now itching to take control of the expedition and therefore were in no hurry to save Magellan's life, but Serrão and Barbosa might have been expected to take some action. No one knows why they did not do so. For whatever reason, while the men who had accompanied Magellan onto the beach panicked and ran away, those who remained in the boats sat idly by and watched the Filipinos cut down his rear guard one by one. At last Carvalho fired a salvo from one of the *Concepción's* guns, but instead of striking Lapulapu it hit Colambu's canoe fleet, by accident or by design, and Colambu promptly withdrew from the scene.

As Pigafetta tells it, Magellan was struck in the arm by a bamboo lance. Seeing Magellan wounded, Lapulapu's men fell upon him, and one of them struck him in the left leg. The captain-general fell face downward. "On this all at once rushed upon him with lances of iron and of bamboo and with these javelins," wrote Pigafetta, "so that they slew our mirror, our light, our comfort, and our true guide." Pigafetta and one or two others escaped to the boats, and Magellan's body was left behind in a few feet of bloody water. It was never recovered.

The captain-general was dead, but three ships and many men remained half a world away from home. Serrão and

Barbosa took command of the fleet and returned to Cebu, where a fresh disaster awaited them. Henrique was to have been freed upon his master's death, but when Barbosa refused to grant him his liberty, Henrique cooked up a plot with Rajah Humabon, whose commitment to Christianity waned after his patron was shown to be less than invincible. Serrão, Barbosa, Carvalho, Espinosa, and 25 others were invited to a feast ashore. After a short while, Carvalho and Espinosa grew suspicious and fled to the ships. Cries were then heard from shore, and Carvalho ordered the guns fired on the town. Soon the rajah's men brought Serrão, bleeding and bound, to the dock. He cried

The trading ships of the Pacific Ocean were easy prey for the explorers-turned-pirates of Magellan's crew after their leader's death in the Philippines.

across the water that all the others, save only Henrique, had been killed by treachery. Serrão then said that the rajah would let him go if Carvalho would send a boat ashore with some merchandise, but Carvalho refused. Says Pigafetta: "Then Serrão, weeping, said that as soon as we sailed he would be killed. And he said that he prayed God that at the day of judgment he would demand his soul of his friend João Carvalho." Carvalho did not relent, and the fleet sailed off, leaving Serrão to an unknown—but probably unkind—fate.

From this point on, the expedition was little more than a renegade adventure. Carvalho and Espinosa took command, but only about 120 men remained—not enough to work 3 ships. They sank the *Concepción* and divided its crew between the *Trinidad* and the *Victoria*, then embarked on a spree of piracy, looting, slaughter, and rape along the length of the Philippine archipelago and south

After nearly 27 months at sea, Magellan's weary fleet landed at Tidore, in the Moluccas, in November 1521, "wherefore," in Pigafetta's words, "we gave thanks to God, and for our great joy we discharged all our artillery."

through the Sulu and Celebes seas, visiting the coast of Borneo several times. On November 6, 1521, 820 days and 28,000 miles (44,800 kilometers) after leaving Seville, they came in sight of the goal they had sought for so long: the Moluccas. Francisco Serrão was dead by now, but the sultan of Tidore welcomed the Spanish and gave them a valuable cargo of cloves and a pair of stuffed birds of paradise.

The *Trinidad* sprang a leak in Tidore while the surviving officers and men were deciding how to get home. Juan Sebastián de Elcano wanted to take the *Victoria* and make for Spain through the Indian Ocean and around the Cape of Good Hope, but this route would have brought the Spanish adventurers into Portuguese waters, where they could expect to receive no mercy from the Portuguese if they were caught trespassing. So Carvalho, Espinosa, and 52 of the men decided instead to repair the *Trinidad* and then retrace their course across the Pacific, hoping to reach Spanish outposts in Panama (Carvalho died in Tidore while the ship was being repaired). The remaining two ships of the fleet therefore separated at Tidore. Trying to reach the Pacific, the men aboard the *Trinidad* encountered crippling storms and dreadful hunger in the cold waters off Japan. They gave up and returned to the Moluccas, where they were captured by the Portuguese. The former flagship was wrecked in a storm near Ternate, and Espinosa and a handful of survivors were imprisoned, first in the Indies and then in Lisbon. Eventually four of them were returned to Seville. The king awarded Espinosa, one of Magellan's most loyal and valiant followers, a high-paying job as inspector of the East Indies fleet. The last known record of him is in 1543, when he still held that well-earned post.

Elcano and the men of the *Victoria's* final crew, which included Pigafetta, are the real circumnavigators of this epic voyage. They left Tidore on December 21, 1521. Just one month later, they left the last of the Spice Islands behind and set off for home. Ahead lay the widest stretch of the Indian Ocean, the cape, and the entire length of West Africa. Elcano planned to make the best possible speed and no landfalls, so as to avoid interception by the Portuguese vessels that plied those seas. He did it, too, despite rotten provisions, lack of water, adverse winds, calms, sickness and death among the crew, and a storm near the Cape of Good Hope that destroyed the *Victoria's* foremast, forcing the ship to limp along at a painfully slow rate of progress. In all, the voyage home was nearly as nightmarish as the Pacific crossing. Finally, in July, desperate for food and water, Elcano landed at the Portuguese-held Cape Verde Islands and managed to sail away just before being apprehended. From Timor in Indonesia to the Cape Verdes was the longest open-sea voyage without a landfall that had ever been made—and one of the most miserable. On September 6, the *Victoria* entered the Guadalquivir River at Sanlúcar de Barrameda, and 2 days later the battered and leaky vessel, with Elcano and 18 starving men aboard, docked in Seville. Fortunately for posterity, Pigafetta was one of the survivors. "And on Tuesday," he wrote at the end of his account, "we all went, in our shirts and barefoot, and each with a torch in his hand, to visit the shrine of Santa María de la Victoria and that of Santa María de Antigua."

The immediate rewards of the voyage were slim: a load of cloves from the *Victoria* that paid for the cost of the expedition but left little profit; a royal pension for Elcano, the former mutineer and master mariner, with a coat of arms that showed a globe wrapped in a motto that read *Primus circumdedisti me* ("Thou first circumnavigated me"); and nothing for Magellan's heirs (his wife had died before 1522, and so had his son Rodrigo). Most of the seamen who returned were still suing the king for back pay years later.

Home at last, Elcano and the others finally learned what had happened to the *San Antonio* after it vanished from

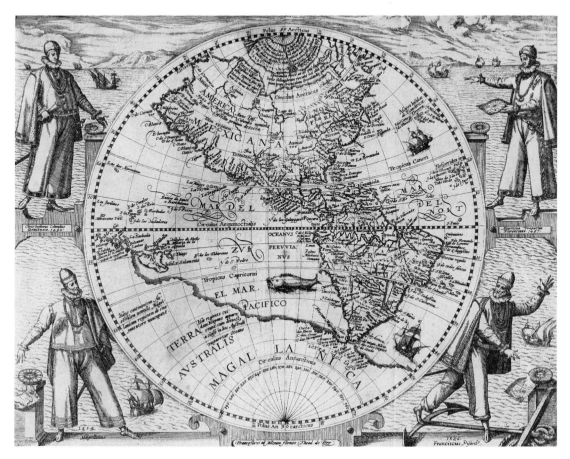

the strait. Upon reaching Spain, Gomes and Guerra had lied about Magellan's conduct of the expedition and had managed to have Alvaro de Mesquita thrown in jail, where he languished until the crew of the *Victoria* arrived to set the record straight. Mesquita was then released, complaining bitterly of Spanish ingratitude; he later returned to Portugal at the invitation of King Manoel.

In the years following 1522, accounts of the voyage were among Europe's best-sellers. Pigafetta completed his in 1524. Another version was prepared by Peter Martyr, an Italian scholar at the Spanish court, who interviewed Elcano and the other survivors at length; his manuscript was sent to Rome, however, and is believed to have been de-

A 1596 map of the New World, which the explorations of Columbus (top left), Vespucci (top right), and Magellan (bottom left) had helped to reveal.

stroyed in an attack on that city in 1527. Fortunately, in 1522 Peter's secretary and pupil, Maximilian of Transylvania, had sent a long letter to his father, the cardinal-archbishop of Salzburg, in which he repeated much of what Peter had learned. This letter was published in several versions over the years. Other accounts, including those of Portuguese historians João de Barros (1552) and Gaspar Correa (1563), drew more or less closely on the stories of the survivors. One way or another, most educated people after the middle of the 16th century came across some version of Magellan's adventures. Yet the Portuguese reviled him as a traitor, and the Spanish gave all the credit for his achievement to Elcano. Only gradually, over time, did Magellan emerge as one of the greatest mariners of a great age of seagoing exploration.

The first chronicler, however, described Magellan best. Wrote Pigafetta to the grand master of the island of Rhodes, to whom his account was dedicated:

The route of Magellan's magnificent voyage is highlighted on this handsome map dating from about 1545. Drawn by the esteemed Genoese cartographer Battista Agnese, the map was part of an atlas presented by Charles I of Spain, Magellan's sponsor, to his son, the future Philip II.

I hope that, by your illustrious lordship, the renown of so
valiant and noble a captain will not be extinguished or fall
into oblivion in our time. For among his other virtues he
was more constant in a very high hazard and great affair
than ever was any other. He endured hunger better than
all the others. He was a navigator and made sea charts.
And that is true was seen openly, for no other had so
much natural wit, boldness, or knowledge to sail once
around the world, as he had undertaken.

Ferdinand Magellan did not complete the voyage he began. He did not even reach his original goal, the Spice
Islands. He found the strait for which many had searched,
but his voyage did not open up a busy new seaway for
trade and colonization, as Columbus's had done. The
passage through the Strait of Magellan was, and is, long,
dangerous, difficult, and expensive. Only a handful of
mariners used it during the following century: Sir Francis
Drake, the Dutchmen Schouten and Le Maire, a few
others. Spain's extensive traffic with its Philippine territory
was carried on through Panama, where cargoes were carried overland from the Pacific fleet to the Atlantic fleet.
Indeed, the strait was so little known that its exact location
was debated for many years, and some people denied its
very existence.

But the passage of time helped Magellan's achievement
gain the stature it deserved, as people gradually grew more
familiar with the size of the world and realized the scope
of what he had done. His discovery of the strait and his
crossing of the Pacific were feats of seamanship that could
inspire others but could never be surpassed. Magellan
proved the truth of what before had only been conjecture—
that the earth is a sphere, and that it can be circumnavigated—and he was the first to see that all the seas of earth
are really one great world ocean, passing endlessly into
one another.

Further Reading

Barclay, William Singer. *The Land of Magellan*. New York: Brentano, 1956.

Beaglehole, J. C. *The Exploration of the Pacific*. London: Charles Black, 1966.

Benson, Edward Frederic. *Ferdinand Magellan*. New York: Harper & Brothers, 1930.

Blackwood, Alan. *Ferdinand Magellan*. New York: Bookwright Press, 1985.

Brownlee, Walter D. *The First Ships Around the World*. Minneapolis: Lerner, 1974.

Cameron, Ian. *Magellan and the First Circumnavigation of the World*. New York: Saturday Review Press, 1973.

Daniel, Hawthorne. *Ferdinand Magellan*. New York: Doubleday, 1964.

Friis, Herman R., ed. *The Pacific Basin: A History of Its Geographical Exploration*. New York: American Geographical Society, 1967.

Guillemard, F. H. H. *The Life of Ferdinand Magellan*. London: G. Philip and Son, 1890.

Markham, Clements R., trans. and ed. *Early Spanish Voyages to the Straits of Magellan*. London: Hakluyt Society, 1911.

Mitchell, Mairin. *Elcano: The First Circumnavigator*. London: Herder Books, 1958.

Morison, Samuel Eliot. *The Great Explorers: The European Discovery of America*. New York: Oxford University Press, 1972.

Nowell, Charles E., ed. *Magellan's Voyage Around the World: Three Contemporary Accounts*. Evanston, IL: Northwestern University Press, 1962.

Ober, Frederick A. *Ferdinand Magellan*. New York: Harper & Brothers, 1907.

Parr, Charles McKew. *"So Noble a Captain": The Life and Times of Ferdinand Magellan*. New York: Crowell, 1953.

Pigafetta, Antonio. *First Around the World: A Journal of Magellan's Voyage*. Edited by George Sanderlin. New York: Harper & Row, 1964.

————. *Magellan's Voyage: A Narrative Account of the First Circumnavigation*, 2 vols. Translated by R. A. Skelton. New Haven, CT: Yale University Press, 1969.

————. *The Philippines*. Translated by Rodrique L'evesque. Gatineau, Quebec: Les Editions L'evesque, 1980.

Pond, Seymour Gates. *Ferdinand Magellan, Master Mariner*. New York: Random House, 1957.

Roditi, Edouard. *Magellan of the Pacific*. New York: McGraw-Hill, 1972.

Silverberg, Robert. *The Longest Voyage: Circumnavigators in the Age of Discovery*. New York: Bobbs-Merrill, 1972.

Syme, Ronald. *Magellan, First Around the World*. New York: Morrow, 1953.

Welch, Ronald. *Ferdinand Magellan*. New York: Criterion Books, 1956.

Wilkie, Katherine Elliott. *Ferdinand Magellan: Noble Captain*. Boston: Houghton Mifflin, 1963.

Zweig, Stefan. *The Story of Magellan*. 1932. Reprint. Philadelphia: Century Bookbindery, 1983.

Chronology

Entries in roman type refer to events directly related to exploration and Magellan's life; entries in italics refer to important historical and cultural events of the era.

1419 — Prince Henry the Navigator becomes governor of southern Portugal and launches the great era of Portuguese sea exploration

1455 — *Johannes Gutenberg prints his famous Bible at Mainz*

1472 — *First edition of Dante's* Divine Comedy *printed*

1478 — *Spanish Inquisition begins*

1480 — Magellan born in northern Portugal

1483 — King João II of Portugal refuses to finance Columbus's proposed voyage westward to the Indies

1487 — Portuguese mariner Bartolomeu Dias rounds Cape of Good Hope

1492 — *The Moors surrender to Ferdinand and Isabella of Spain*; Columbus makes the first of his four voyages to the Americas; Magellan begins service as a page in the royal court of Portugal

1494 — Pope Alexander VI proclaims the Treaty of Tordesillas, which divides the New World between Portugal and Spain

1495 — Manoel I (the Fortunate) becomes king of Portugal; *Leonardo da Vinci begins* The Last Supper

1497–99 — Portuguese seaman Vasco da Gama commands the first European expedition to reach India by sea, enabling Portugal to begin its Asian conquests; John Cabot, sailing for England, reaches shores of North America; Magellan employed in the Casa da India in Lisbon

1500 — Pedro Álvars Cabral discovers Brazil and claims it for Portugal

1502 — After making two voyages there, Amerigo Vespucci concludes that South America is a separate continent

1505–13	Magellan sails with the armada of Francisco de Almeida to Africa and India, where he remains for eight years, rising to the rank of captain and possibly voyaging as far east as the Banda Sea or the Philippines; *Michelangelo paints the ceiling of the Sistine Chapel*
1508	*European powers and the church unite against Venice in the League of Cambrai*
1513–14	Magellan serves in King Manoel's Moroccan campaign, is court-martialed, and is dismissed from Manoel's service; Spanish explorer Vasco Núñez de Balboa crosses the Isthmus of Panama and looks out upon the Pacific Ocean, which he calls the South Sea; Spanish explorer Ponce de León discovers Florida
1517	*Martin Luther posts his 95 Theses on the door of the Palast Church in Wittenberg, ushering in the Reformation*; Magellan leaves Portugal and offers his services to Spain
1518	Magellan marries Beatriz, daughter of Diogo Barbosa; King Charles I of Spain names Magellan captain-general of a fleet of five ships to be used to discover a new route to the Indies
1519	Magellan's fleet sets sail for the Indies; Spanish conqueror Hernán Cortés captures Tenochtitlán, the Aztec capital, and holds Aztec king Montezuma hostage
1520	Magellan discovers the strait that bears his name; his fleet enters the Pacific Ocean in November
1521	Magellan killed in battle with native inhabitants of the Philippines in April; his nemesis, King Manoel I of Portugal, dies in December
1522	One ship of Magellan's fleet, the *Victoria*, captained by Juan Sebastián de Elcano and manned by 18 men, arrives in Spain to conclude the first circumnavigation of the world

Index

Picture Credits

Rebecca Stefoff holds a Ph.D. in English from the University of Pennsylvania, where she taught from 1974 to 1977. The author of many works of fiction and nonfiction, she currently serves as editorial director of the Chelsea House series PLACES AND PEOPLES OF THE WORLD, to which she has contributed the volume *West Bank/Gaza Strip*. She is also the author of *Yasir Arafat* and *Faisal* in the Chelsea House series WORLD LEADERS—PAST & PRESENT.

William H. Goetzmann holds the Jack S. Blanton, Sr., Chair in History at the University of Texas at Austin, where he has taught for many years. The author of numerous works on American history and exploration, he won the 1967 Pulitzer and Parkman prizes for his *Exploration and Empire: The Role of the Explorer and Scientist in the Winning of the American West, 1800–1900*. With his son William N. Goetzmann, he coauthored *The West of the Imagination*, which received the Carr P. Collins Award in 1986 from the Texas Institute of Letters. His documentary television series of the same name received a blue ribbon in the history category at the American Film and Video Festival held in New York City in 1987. A recent work, *New Lands, New Men: America and the Second Great Age of Discovery*, was published in 1986 to much critical acclaim.

Michael Collins served as command module pilot on the *Apollo 11* space mission, which landed his colleagues Neil Armstrong and Buzz Aldrin on the moon. A graduate of the United States Military Academy, Collins was named an astronaut in 1963. In 1966 he piloted the *Gemini 10* mission, during which he became the third American to walk in space. The author of several books on space exploration, Collins was director of the Smithsonian Institution's National Air and Space Museum from 1971 to 1978 and is a recipient of the Presidential Medal of Freedom.